3903

Y. A
B
B- GUR
C. 3

Congregation Shaare Shamayim-G.N.J.C.

In Memory of

Dedicated By

Bea Cardonick

David Ben-Gurion

DAVID BEN-GURION

by Herma Silverstein

3903

FRANKLIN WATTS | 1988
NEW YORK | LONDON | SYDNEY | TORONTO
AN IMPACT BIOGRAPHY

Photographs courtesy of: The Bettmann Archive, Inc.: pp. 2, 67, 85;
Culver Pictures, Inc.: pp. 14, 28, 42, 50; UPI/Bettmann Newsphotos:
pp. 62, 96, 101; AP/Wide World Photos: pp. 80, 106, 117.

Library of Congress Cataloging in Publication Data

Silverstein, Herma.
David Ben-Gurion.

(An Impact Biography)
Bibliography: p.
Includes index.
Summary: Surveys the life and career of the first
prime minister of Israel.
1. Ben-Gurion, David, 1886–1973—Juvenile literature.
2. Prime ministers—Israel—Biography—Juvenile
literature.   3. Zionists—Palestine—Biography—
Juvenile literature.   [1. Ben-Gurion, David,
1886–1973.   2. Prime ministers.   3. Zionists.
4. Israel—History]
DS125.3.B37S55   1988   956.94′05′0924 [2] [92]   87–21635
ISBN 0-531-10509-1

IN LOVING MEMORY OF
BEN E. ELLMAN
AND
SARA D. ELLMAN

Contents

David Ben-Gurion

ONE

★

The Young Goliath

They shall beat their swords into plowshares,
and their spears into pruning hooks:
nation shall not lift up sword against nation,
neither shall they learn war any more.

Isaiah 2:4

The passengers sweltered from the hot sun as the caravan wedged its way through the traffic on Rothschild Street. The sixty-two-year-old man in the lead car dabbed his handkerchief across his cheeks, tanned and leathery now from living so many years in the desert. Finally the caravan stopped in front of the Tel Aviv Museum of Art. The man got out of the car, and hundreds of Jews crowding outside the museum burst into cheers. He waved, then went inside and joined his colleagues behind a dais in front of the auditorium.

At exactly four o'clock, the man stepped up to a microphone, and the audience shrank into silence. He removed a piece of paper from his jacket and started to read. The paper was the Declaration of Independence of the State of Israel. When he finished reading, shouts of "Mazel Tov" rose above the thunderous applause. The man's blue eyes filled with tears. His speech had been short compared to the long road the Jews had traveled to arrive at this day— May 14, 1948. After almost two thousand years of persecution and exile, the Jews had finally reclaimed their ancient homeland, *Eretz Israel*, the Land of Israel.

The man everyone cheered was the first prime minister of Israel, the person most responsible for its rebirth. His name was David Ben-Gurion, and he had come a long way from his youth in a Jewish ghetto in Poland.

David Ben-Gurion was born David Gruen, or Green, on October 16, 1886, in the village of Plonsk, Poland, then part of the Russian Empire. Czar Alexander III ruled the empire, and like his predecessors, he was a tyrannical anti-Semite. The czar allowed Jews to live only in the southwestern region of the empire, known as the "Pale of Settlement." Within each village, Jews were restricted to living in a section known as the "Jewish Quarter." Although the Jews could move freely about the town, they needed a permit to travel outside the Pale. In addition, Jewish homes were raided, their property was confiscated, and their books were censored.

Even worse, Russian Jews lived in fear of anti-Semitic attacks called *pogroms*. During a pogrom, non-Jewish mobs went on a rampage, burning Jewish homes, vandalizing their shops, and killing Jews. The czars encouraged pogroms whenever they needed someone to blame for Russia's economic and political problems.

To escape persecution, many Eastern European Jews joined a new movement, called Zionism. The Zionists believed that the biblical land of Israel should be won back by the Jews through work and improvement of the land. In 70 A.D., the Romans had conquered the land of Judea and its provinces. They exiled the Jews and renamed the area Palestine. The Jews dispersed, or separated, to resettle in different parts of the world. Their separation from Israel and scattering over the world is known as the *Diaspora*.

David's father, Avigdor Green, was a supporter of Zionism and belonged to one of the first Zionist organizations established in Eastern Europe, called the "Lovers of Zion." The purpose of this group was to find a way to make Zionisms's goal a reality. An early attempt had been made in 1882 when a group of Russian students emigrated to Palestine and started recultivating a section of barren land there. These first immigrants were helped by Jewish philanthropists such as Sir Moses Montefiore of England, whose donations helped Jews plant their first orange grove in Palestine.

Another wealthy Jew, the Frenchman Baron Edmond de Rothschild, formed the Jewish Colonization Association, which negotiated with Palestinian Arab landowners to buy portions of their land in Palestine. The association gave the land to Jewish immigrants to settle on and farm. The Jews made a little progress recultivating the soil, much of which was barren desert, but there were not enough of them to rebuild an entire country. As more Jews emigrated to Palestine, their journey became known as *aliyah*, from the Hebrew word meaning "going up."

In support of *aliyah* and Zionism, David's father held nightly meetings of the Lovers of Zion in his home. His father was so involved in these meetings that he had little time for David, or David's older brothers, and sister, Avraham, Michael and Rivka. As a toddler, David wandered in and out of these meetings. His job was to collect three rubles from everyone there to be sent to Zionist headquarters in Odessa. Each night after David's mother put him to bed, he would lie awake listening through his open door to the men talk.

"I didn't understand much," David said, "but somehow it [Zionism] got into my blood."[1] Countless times he heard the men repeat one phrase, *Eretz Israel*. By the time David

was a teenager, he believed his destiny would somehow be wrapped up in *Eretz Israel*.

When David was three, Avigdor's father, Zvi Aryeh, started teaching the young boy Hebrew. He would climb on his grandfather's lap, and Zvi Aryeh would point to different pieces of furniture and say their Hebrew words. David would repeat the words. Zvi Aryeh was amazed at David's incredible memory. Within a short time, he knew the Hebrew word for every piece of furniture in the house.

By the time David was old enough to attend Hebrew school, he understood more of what the Zionists talked about at his father's nightly meetings. He started to believe that the Jewish state the Zionists spoke of was essential if Jews were ever to escape anti-Semitic persecution. On his first day of school, David shocked his classmates by announcing that one day he would be "the first king of Israel in modern times."[2]

His teacher thought David was extremely bright for his age and recommended that he be moved into the class for gifted students, in the *Bet Hamidrash*, or House of Study. David loved the new class. There he developed a love of reading that would become his only way to ease the tensions of running a newly created government when he later became prime minister of Israel.

While growing up, David was more fortunate than most other children in Plonsk, who lived in dilapidated wooden houses facing dirty cobblestone alleys. David's father made

Avigdor Green, David Ben-Gurion's father, a lawyer and member of the local Hovevei Zion (Lovers of Zion) in the Polish village of Plonsk. From his father, David inherited his love for the Jewish people and his passionate commitment to Zionism.

a decent living as an unlicensed lawyer. When he married David's mother, Sheindel, her father gave Avigdor a tract of land on the outskirts of Plonsk as part of her marriage dowry. Avigdor bought good timber and built a sturdy two-story house on the land.

For all of David's good fortune, until he was about nine years old, he was thin and often sick. As a result, he could not play outdoor games with other boys his age. When his health finally improved, the neighborhood boys started asking David to join in their games. But David had never learned how to play these games. He was afraid the boys would laugh at him if he tried to play and failed, so he told them that he felt childhood games were a waste of time. The only game he would play was chess, which his father taught him when he was six years old. David could beat people twice his age. He had the ability to concentrate on his next move for hours without getting bored or distracted.

Although David was normally shy, he occasionally wanted to prove he was one of the gang. At these times the mischievous little boy in him came out, and he would join the other children in pulling pranks. A favorite prank was stealing fruit off the trees in neighbors' yards.

When David was ten, a tragedy occurred that affected him the rest of his life. His mother died while giving birth to her eleventh child. David was crushed. He adored his mother, and she (Sheindel) had cherished him. She never hid the fact that she loved David and his brother Avraham the best of all her children. Sheindel was always saying, "My son Avraham will be the greatest Jewish scholar in this town; but my little son David—the whole world will call him great."[3]

For several years after his mother's death, David was so depressed that he felt as if life had no meaning for him. "I used to see her in my dreams regularly, for almost two years," he said. "I would . . . ask her why she did not come back."[4]

David numbed his pain by hiding his deepest feelings

inside himself. The only way he could express his personal feelings was to write them down. He started to keep a diary, which he kept up the rest of his life. He also wrote long letters to his friends. Writing his feelings down released some of David's pent-up sadness.

While he acted happy in front of others, David was lonely. He tried to find a substitute for his mother's love by becoming closer to his father. David started attending Avigdor's Zionist meetings regularly. Soon he started asking questions and offering his own opinions. By the time he was a teenager, David knew he wanted to emigrate to Palestine and work to build *Eretz Israel*. Establishing a Jewish national homeland in Palestine became David Green's dream. He grew so obsessed with this goal that he never again put anyone or anything ahead of achieving his dream.

When David was twelve, he no longer wanted to study the Talmud, the Jewish laws and tradition, which were required in Hebrew school. His father gave him permission to change to a public secondary school. This was the first time David had been in a classroom with girls. One of the girls in particular caught his eye. She was Rachel Nelkin. David thought she was the most beautiful girl in Plonsk, with long eyelashes that shaded her big brown eyes and shiny dark hair braided down her back. Yet David was so shy he was afraid to talk to Rachel.

Two years later, David's best friend, Shlomo Zemach, convinced him otherwise. David had grown into a handsome fourteen-year-old, with shocks of dark curly hair and sparkling blue eyes. Many young girls in Plonsk had crushes on him. David, however, seemed to be blind to all girls except Rachel. Then Shlomo found out that Rachel had as big a crush on David as he had on her, and insisted that David ask Rachel to go for a walk with him. David took Shlomo's advice, and soon David and Rachel were a couple. They shared a silent love for each other, however, as the emotional barrier that David had put between himself and others he cared about kept him from telling Rachel how he felt about her.

Yet being with Rachel often brought out the mischievous little boy in David. At these times he changed from a shy adolescent into a teenage rebel. David would ask Rachel out for a walk and insist they go without a chaperone, which was frowned upon in the early twentieth century. No *decent* young girl, the villagers gossiped, would go out *alone* with a gentleman.

A few months later David formed a boy's Zionist youth group in Plonsk, called the Ezra Society. Its original purpose was to promote Hebrew as a spoken language. Eventually David turned the society into a Jewish self-defense force, complete with members wearing khaki uniforms and pistols bulging out of their belts. David felt so impressive in his uniform that he often acted like a little boy playing soldier. Whenever he saw Rachel ride by in a carriage, he would shoot his gun into the air, hoping she would notice how brave he looked. The villagers started ducking whenever they saw him coming. Fortunately David Green was an excellent shot.[5]

During this time, David met the man who would most influence him to continue to devote his life to Zionism. The man was Theodor Herzl, a Hungarian-born Jew, who had been a reporter for an Austrian newspaper. In 1894, Herzl covered the court-martial trial of French army captain Alfred Dreyfus, a Jew who was accused of treason. When Dreyfus was found guilty, Herzl was horrified by the anti-Semitic testimony given at the trial. Until then, Herzl had not been aware of the degree of anti-Semitism in Europe and had been only a dabbler in Zionism. He now joined the movement wholeheartedly.

In 1896 Herzl published a book titled *The Jewish State,* calling for the founding of a Jewish homeland. The next year he invited Jewish representatives from all over the world to meet in Basel, Switzerland. Through Herzl's leadership, they formed the World Zionist Organization (WZO). Herzl declared the aim of the organization was to achieve "a publicly recognized and legally secured Jewish home in Palestine."[6] When Theodor Herzl visited Plonsk,

David thought the tall man with the black beard falling down to his chest looked like the Messiah himself. "One glimpse of him," David remembered, "and I was ready to follow him then and there to the land of my ancestors."[7]

Herzl negotiated with world leaders to get them to issue a charter establishing a Jewish homeland. David was inspired by Herzl's role in the founding of Zionism, and started giving his own Zionist speeches to large groups of Jews. David's ability to speak intelligently and with a tone of authority made adults listen to him. "Words without deeds are nothing . . ." he told his audiences. "One must show the way by example. . . ."[8] In the meantime, David grew impatient waiting for Herzl's charter to materialize. He decided that the way for Jews to reclaim their ancient land was by their own physical labor in rebuilding that land. "By creating something fruitful where previously there was nothing."[9]

In 1903, when the Sixth World Zionist Congress met in Basel, Theodor Herzl reported to the delegates that the sultan of Turkey, whose Ottoman Empire embraced much of the Middle East, including Palestine, had rejected his proposal to let Jews build a homeland in Palestine. Great Britain then offered Jews territory in Kenya, a British colony in Africa, for their homeland. Herzl mistakenly called the colony Uganda, and Jews everywhere debated the "Uganda Issue."

Some Zionists favored establishing a Jewish state anywhere, so long as they could live in freedom. Others, like David Green, were against the idea. What would a Jewish state be without Israel? they asked. David determined to fight the British offer by having members of the Ezra Society emigrate to Palestine and start rebuilding the land to prepare the way for other Jews to follow. He longed to go with the Ezra members who were selected to emigrate first, but his father insisted that David get his high school diploma before he left. Although David was disappointed, he felt he must respect his father's wishes.

A year later, however, the question of David's emigration faded into the background as Czar Nicolas II, who had succeeded Alexander III in 1894, ordered a new wave of pogroms throughout Russia. An especially hideous pogrom occurred in 1903 in Kishinev, the capital of the Russian province of Bessarabia. Peasant mobs burst into Jewish homes and butchered everyone inside. The massacres at Kishinev sickened David. At the same time, he was furious with the Jews there for allowing themselves to be slaughtered without putting up a fight.

David called the Jews in Plonsk to a meeting at the synagogue. With his voice shaking, David begged them to arm themselves and fight back if a pogrom occurred in Plonsk. The Jews were shocked. No one had ever dared suggest rebelling against the czar. Russian officials might be lurking outside, just waiting to arrest one of them for spouting ideas of rebellion.

Unafraid, David started to give speeches for the creation of a Jewish defense force in Plonsk. During one of his speeches, the rabbi interrupted him, afraid that one of the czar's secret police might be listening through the synagogue door. The rabbi shouted that all Jews were loyal to the czar and none was a revolutionary. David was stunned by the rabbi's lie. He shouted back that the czar's laws were pushing the Jews into rebellion in the first place. Furthermore, if the adults were too afraid to take action, he and other Jewish boys his age would. True to his word, David turned the Ezra Society into a Jewish self-defense force. Soon the boys were smuggling weapons into David's house. He believed that even if they were killed, at least they would die fighting.[10]

In 1904 Theodor Herzl died. David again felt as though his world had ended. As usual, he expressed his innermost feelings with pen and ink rather than with spoken words. He wrote to a friend about his sorrow: "There will not again arise such a marvelous man. . . . But . . . I have faith in and am certain of our victory. It is clear to me that there is a day—a day that is not far off—when we shall return to that wondrous land . . . of the visionaries' visions."[11]

Adding to David's general depression was his relationship with Rachel, which was not going well. David felt his involvement with her was taking too much time away from the pursuit of his dream. He decided if he lived away from her for a while, he would have a better chance of sorting out his mixed loyalties. That winter, David moved to Warsaw, where he planned to finish high school and then attend a technical college. He would major in engineering to develop skills that were needed to rebuild the land of Israel.

In Warsaw, David found a job teaching Hebrew. Then he went to enroll in high school, and was surprised when the administrator said the Warsaw schools had already filled their "Jewish quotas" for that year. Not giving up, David next applied to a technical college. This time he was turned down for not having a high school diploma, even though he passed the entrance exam with higher marks than non-Jewish students who were admitted.

David was experiencing firsthand the prejudice against Jews that he had only heard about before. Now he knew how other Jews felt when they were refused a seat on a bus, a table at a restaurant, or a room to rent. David felt inhuman when he saw the signs posted around Warsaw saying, "No Jews or Dogs Allowed." More and more he believed the only way Jews would ever escape such hatred was to live in a land of their own, where they would be welcomed.

Meanwhile, the Seventh World Zionist Congress in 1905, had declared that a Jewish homeland *must* be established in Palestine, thus vetoing the Uganda Proposal. In Warsaw, David joined a new Zionist movement called the *Po'alei Zion* ("The Workers of Zion"). The party's goal was to build a socialist state in Palestine where everyone would share the work and the wealth. Members proposed to form local Po'alei Zion branches in other European cities, and organize the workers. David jumped at the chance to form a Po'alei Zion branch in Plonsk, as he would have an excuse to see Rachel again. Living away from her had not helped him come to any conclusion about their relationship other than that he loved her more than ever. When David arrived in Plonsk, he was relieved to hear from Rachel that her feelings for him also had not changed.

Happy once again, David concentrated on his job. First he converted members of the Ezra Society into a branch of the Po'alei Zion. Then, by explaining their rights to local workers, he succeeded in organizing seamstresses, housemaids, and employees of a knitting shop. David was amazed at the power of organized labor. He realized that a united labor movement could be a powerful tool in Palestine to help establish the Jewish state. If he could not become an engineer in Palestine, he would become a labor leader.

Filled with enthusiasm, David decided he would make his *aliyah* as soon as he could get a visa. He convinced his father to give him his blessing, if not his agreement, since Avigdor still believed his son should first finish his education. Then Rachel told David she was emigrating, too, and she and her mother would be sailing on the same ship as David. Rachel's stepfather had gone ahead to find a place for them to live. Now David was doubly overjoyed to be going to Palestine.

Thus in the summer of 1906, nineteen-year-old David Green boarded the Russian freighter that would take him to Palestine. With him were Shlomo Zemach, Rachel, and her mother. To David, his life was just beginning. Finally he could actively work to build a Jewish homeland and fulfill his dream. Years later, David would look back upon this day and reflect that his belief that emigrating would make his dream come true almost as soon as his feet touched Palestinian soil, had been merely the naïveté of youth. For when David Green said good-bye to his family that summer day in 1906, he never imagined that he would spend the next forty-two years fighting malaria, starvation, and Arab resistance before his dream would ever come true.

TWO

★

Aliyah at Last

David winced as another passenger on the overcrowded freighter stepped on his foot. He tried to make some elbow room on the deck, which served as their living quarters for the fourteen-day journey to Palestine. But people and animals were pressed together like sardines in a can. Several of the Arabs on board had even brought their camels with them. Yet David's mind swam with so many thoughts about Palestine that he barely noticed the filth surrounding him, caused in part by the crew, who refused to clean the deck after the Jews. The stench of sweat and defecation filled the air, and the sounds of retching could be heard at all hours. While Shlomo Zemach seemed to brave the discomfort with no ill effects, Rachel and her mother had trouble keeping down even one mouthful of food.

During the journey, David was surprised by the friendliness of the Arabs on board. He reasoned that if these Moslems were typical of the ones living in Palestine, then the Jews should have no problem getting along with them. The night before they docked, David stared out over the Mediterranean Sea, searching for his first sight of land. He wrote in his diary that, "I was sure even then that this land would become entirely Jewish. I knew we had here the opportunity and the mettle to prove ourselves entirely Jewish."[1]

The next morning, when Palestine came into view, David could barely stop himself from jumping overboard and swimming the rest of the way. ". . . I stood and gazed at Jaffa," he said. "And my heart was beating wildly . . . I had arrived."[2] But when David Green actually set foot on the soil of the "Promised Land," he almost never took a second step. David, Shlomo, Rachel, and her mother stared in bewildered horror at the village at the end of the dock.

Jaffa was a poor town, seemingly left to rot since the Turks had conquered Palestine four hundred years earlier. Emaciated beggars swarmed around them like mosquitoes. Arabs wearing torn robes led camels down alleys littered with dung. In the distance, instead of the orange groves and beautiful countryside David had imagined, all he saw was an endless sea of sand and sagebrush. David could not get out of Jaffa fast enough. He felt impatient to go on to Petah Tikvah ("The Gate of Hope"), the oldest village of the twenty Jewish settlements then in Palestine. Rachel's parents intended to settle in Petah Tikvah, and David and Shlomo hoped to find jobs there.

While waiting for Rachel's stepfather to come to the dock, they met a group of young immigrants who were also going to Petah Tikvah. Among them was Israel Schochat, who would become David's good friend. David and Shlomo decided to walk to Petah Tikvah with Israel Shochat and the immigrants. Rachel wanted to go with David. She arranged to stay in Petah Tikvah with friends from Plonsk who had emigrated there earlier, while her parents followed by carriage a few days later. When Rachel's stepfather arrived at the dock, he and Rachel's mother went to stay at his hotel, while David, Shlomo, and Rachel set off with the other immigrants. David bought a mule for the three of them to take turns riding.

When they reached Petah Tikvah, David wondered what was so "hopeful" about the village. The sun beat down unmercifully on the wooden huts that housed the settlement's two hundred and fifty Jews. Cypress trees provided the only shade from the withering heat. David and Shlomo left Rachel at her friends' hut while they went job-hunting. After three days, they were still unemployed, and David considered returning to Jaffa. Then they ran into a classmate from Plonsk who was a friend of a farm manager. He persuaded the manager to hire David, Shlomo, and Rachel.

Thus David Green began his illustrious career in Palestine on a farm. His job, along with Shlomo and Rachel, was to carry tin cans of manure to the farm's orange groves, pour the manure into holes in the ground, and return for another canful while laborers planted orange tree saplings in the holes. Rachel, unaccustomed to manual labor, cried out in pain as the can's wire handles cut into her palms. She struggled for days to keep working. Her hands became raw and bled whenever she lifted the can. Finally Rachel had to stop working, and the overseer fired her.

That night, while the workers gathered together to eat dinner, the laborers from Plonsk lashed out at Rachel for making them look weak. She burst into tears. David's torn loyalty between Rachel and his dream resurfaced when he saw her sitting on the ground, seemingly helpless. He realized if they married now he might have to divide his time between taking care of Rachel's needs and those of Zionism. If he had to choose, David knew his choice would be *Eretz Israel*. He decided to block out his love for Rachel by distancing himself from her until he fulfilled his dream. Rachel was hurt by David's coldness. When one of her old boyfriends from Plonsk, Yehezkel Beit-Halachmi, who also worked on the farm, tried to comfort her, Rachel offered no objection.

David, meanwhile, did not want to be considered weak by the other laborers. He tilled the fields, helped drain the mosquito-infested swamps, and dug boulders out of the ground, which he carried to rock quarries. His clothes tore, his hands blistered, and his muscles strained to the breaking point. Finally David's overexertion weakened his resistance to disease, and he caught malaria. Alternating attacks of chills and high fever plagued him. When his fever rose to 104 degrees, he became delirious. A physician said if he stayed in Palestine, he would die. David declared that if he had to die, it would be in *Eretz Israel*.

To make matters worse, David was fired for missing work. He spent the little money he had on food, which usually amounted to one pita bread a day. "It was bearable during the day," he said, "but at night . . . as soon as I shut my eyes I would imagine pots full of meat . . . plates full of food. . . . In the morning I would feel my head and clumps of hair would drop out and stick to my fingers."[3]

Rachel offered to take care of David, but he refused, afraid he would give in to his emotions and ask her to marry him then. Once again Rachel turned to Yehezkel Beit-Halachmi to soothe her hurt feelings. Moreover, the further David pulled away from Rachel, the closer Yehezkel Beit-Halachmi moved.

After David recovered from malaria, he spent the next year working for the Petah Tikvah branch of the Po'alei Zion party. He was elected to the party's platform committee and to its ruling central committee. In the summer of 1907, he attended a Po'alei Zion conference in Jaffa. He was disappointed when his proposal to make Hebrew the official language of the future Jewish state was vetoed. Most members of the Po'alei Zion party believed that Hebrew was for reading the Torah, and that Yiddish, a mixture of middle high German and a little Polish, should remain the Jew's everyday language.

One of the few members who supported David was Israel Shochat, the immigrant David had met in Jaffa. Another was Yitzhak Shamshelevich, better known as Yitzhak Ben-Zvi, who would become David's most cherished friend, possibly the only true friend David would ever have.

He did gain two victories, however, when his proposals were accepted to unite Palestinian laborers and to merge all Zionist parties in Palestine. David believed that a united Jewish front would be vital when the time came to ask the sultan for permission to establish the Jewish state.

After the Po'alei Zion conference, David found a job at a winery in Rishon LeZion, a village south of Haifa. Each morning he put on a sack with holes in it for his head and arms, then climbed into a huge vat filled with grapes. All day he treaded back and forth squashing grapes. One afternoon David went into town where he ran into Shlomo Zemach. Shlomo had moved north to the Sejera region of the Galilee. He described the beauty of the Galilee and the abundance of jobs there, since the Sejera was the only region in Palestine that hired only Jews. David thought this place sounded exactly like the Palestine he had dreamed about in Plonsk. He decided to move there when Shlomo returned.

First, however, David went to Petah Tikvah to say good-bye to Rachel. He found her sick with malaria and he yearned to stay and take care of her. But he steeled himself not to let his love for her postpone his move. Instead, he rushed off to the Galilee with Shlomo. They found jobs working on a pioneer farm, where David was assigned the task of plowing.

David was surprised by how much he enjoyed walking across the fields behind the oxen. As usual, unable to express his feelings out loud, he wrote them in his diary: "I look on those days as perhaps the best of my life, when I felt everything I was doing had a purpose in the cause of building our new country."[4]

David had been working on the farm only a short time when his world caved in. An immigrant arrived from Petah Tikvah with the news that Rachel was engaged to marry Yehezkel Beit-Halachmi, her old boyfriend from Plonsk. David rushed back to Petah Tikvah to get Rachel to change her mind. He was so desperate he finally told Rachel he loved her and begged her to marry him. David asked her

*David (first row, center) as a young pioneer
farm worker at Rishon LeZion, a village
south of Haifa, Palestine, in 1905.*

just to wait until he fulfilled his dream. Rachel was tired of playing second-best to David's destiny. She told him he did not need a wife; he was already married to his dream.

Depressed and frustrated, David returned to the Sejera farm where he received more bad news. A letter from his father said David had been drafted into the Russian army. According to law, his father would be charged three hundred rubles if David did not show up to enlist.

David's return to Plonsk was not pleasant. He was filled with memories of Rachel and of his mother. Before going to enlist, he went to the cemetery and placed fresh flowers on his mother's grave. After serving a few weeks in the Russian army, David could not tolerate pledging allegiance to the czar one more time. David deserted the army and fled to Warsaw, where he hid out until he could book passage to Palestine. By the beginning of 1908 he was back at the pioneer farm in the Sejera.

At this time, Jewish settlements in Palestine were often attacked by marauding bands of Arabs. David wanted to organize a Jewish defense group as he had done in Plonsk. The farm manager refused, saying that Circassian Russians were already hired to guard the farm. David knew the Circassians were unreliable. To prove his point, he and some other workers played a trick on the manager. That night, they hid one of the manager's mules, then woke up the manager shouting that his mule had been stolen. The manager ran to ask the guard if he had seen any Arabs lurking around, only to find the man sound asleep. The Circassian guards were fired, and David organized his defense force.

Thus the first *shomer*, the Hebrew word for "watchman," was organized in Palestine. Soon the Sejera farmers united with other Jewish farmers to form a self-defense network known as *Hashomer*. David wrote in his diary that Hashomer "removed the reproach of cowardice from the Jews of the country, and enhanced their honor in their own eyes and the eyes of their neighbors."[5]

Hashomer volunteers proved themselves highly capable when an Arab tribe attacked the farm one night. The defense group successfully fought off the Arabs, although two Jews were killed in the battle. David's opinion made on the Russian freighter, that Jews and Arabs should have no trouble getting along together, was obviously wrong. "It was then I realized the wider implications of this small clash," he said. "Sooner or later, Jews and Arabs would fight over this land."[6]

After the Arab attack, the farm manager felt that negotiating with the Arabs would cost less lives than fighting them. He ordered David to disband Hashomer. After another year spent trying, without much success, to organize Jewish workers, David left the Sejera region for good. For two days he walked across the scorching desert toward Jaffa. Once there, David stopped to attend a Po'alei Zion conference, but he was so exhausted he fell onto the bed in his hotel room and slept for twenty-four hours.

David awoke to find Yitzhak Ben-Zvi, the Po'alei Zion member who had supported his "Hebrew language" proposal, standing by his bed. Ben-Zvi was now an editor for *Ahdut* (Unity), a monthly Hebrew-language journal in Jerusalem. He offered David a job writing editorials for the journal, saying that editorials had proved a successful way to publicize the Zionists' goals for a Jewish state. Ben-Zvi sparked David's interest. Maybe if Jewish workers read articles promoting labor unity in a respected Jewish journal, they would feel less afraid of change and consent to organize into unions. David accepted the job.

Before moving to Jerusalem, David visited Rachel, who now lived with her husband and infant daughter near Petah Tikvah. David found Rachel in the living room nursing her baby. He kissed her hello, and she did not seem embarrassed. They spent the afternoon talking as if nothing had changed between them. When David returned to Jaffa, he wrote Rachel asking her to visit him. She never answered. Although David was hurt by Rachel's rejection, he believed he could win her back after he accomplished his dream. David then moved to Jerusalem.

He was disheartened to find that Jerusalem was another sprawling slum, inhabited by the poor of every nationality. David rented a cellar room with several poor art students. After paying his part of the rent, he had only enough money left over for one meal a day. To get his mind off his hunger, David took long walks at night composing editorials in his head. Back in the cellar, he wrote the editorials, then slept until it was time to eat his one meal the next day.

While working for *Adhut*, David Green became David Ben-Gurion. It was the custom for Zionists to change their last names to those of biblical heroes. David chose the name Ben-Gurion in memory of a Jewish hero named Yosef Ben-Gurion, who had died fighting the Romans in 70 A.D. "We were in effect," David said, "indicating our purpose of taking up where they [our Jewish ancestors] left off."[7] This custom still exists in Israel today.

David worked hard for *Ahdut*, and within a year the journal's subscriptions increased enough to change *Ahdut* from a monthly into a weekly journal. The editors decided on three platforms for *Ahdut*: to unify Palestine's Jews, to create a workers' syndicate, and to obtain Jewish autonomy from the Ottoman Empire.

The Ottoman Empire was in a state of chaos. The sultan had been deposed, and in a series of military coups, the young Turks kept overthrowing each other to become the sultan's successor. Each new leader called for the support of minorities, whom they even allowed to run for parliament. Through his editorials, Ben-Gurion urged Palestinian Jews to show their loyalty to the new rulers by becoming Turkish citizens and by running for parliament. Then the Jews could vote for each other and most likely win. That way, enough Jews might be elected into the Turkish parliament to propose, and pass, a motion for the creation of a Jewish state.

David, Yitzhak Ben-Zvi, and Israel Shochat prepared

themselves to run for parliament by studying law the following year at the University of Constantinople (now Istanbul). In the meantime, they planned to attend the Third Congress of the World Union of the Po'alei Zion party, scheduled for July 1911, in Vienna, Austria.

On the way to Vienna, David planned to stop in Lodz, Poland, to see his family. He could hardly wait. David wished the reunion could be in Plonsk, for he was desperate to see Rachel again, who was recuperating there from another bout of malaria. But the Russians in Plonsk still had a warrant out for his arrest for deserting from the army. Therefore, David wrote Rachel asking her to meet him in Lodz, where David's sister, Rivka, lived with her husband.

In June 1911, David Ben-Gurion stepped off the train in Warsaw and threw himself into his family's arms. This homecoming was far happier than his last one, when he faced enlistment in the Russian army. David and his sisters and brothers joked, reminisced, and seemed unable to stop laughing. While traveling by carriage to Lodz, David asked about Rachel. Even though his sisters told him she was happily married and had recently given birth to another daughter, David still believed she loved him.

When Rivka gave a reception in his honor, David asked her to invite Rachel. David practically floated around Rivka's house in anticipation. Then Rachel declined the invitation. David wrote her a letter begging her to meet him in Lodz. This time Rachel answered. Her answer was no. David was heartbroken. He felt encouraged, however, by Rachel's having enclosed a photograph of herself. David kept the photograph the rest of his life.

In July, David attended the Po'alei Zion conference in Vienna, where he was elected to the party's executive committee, pushing him to the forefront of the Zionist movement. Yet even this achievement did not take his mind off Rachel. For the first time in his life, he became afraid that he would never win her back. David wrote her another letter begging her to leave her husband and come to America with him. They could be married in the United States. Rachel never answered his letter, and David, filled with despair, resumed his job at *Ahdut.*

Then David's plans to enter law school in Constantinople were delayed. During the summer of 1912, the Greeks invaded Turkey and the Balkan War erupted in the Middle East. The university closed its doors to serve as a hospital for the wounded. When the war ended in March 1913, Turkey had lost some territories to Greece, but retained Palestine.

Finally David and his colleagues could enter law school in Constantinople, where Ben-Gurion passed his courses with high marks. Before beginning their third term in law school, he and Ben-Zvi decided to take a short vacation in Palestine. On July 28, 1914, as they sailed toward Jaffa aboard a Russian ship, sirens suddenly shrieked and sailors dashed to their defense stations. David's heart nearly stopped. Two German warships were chasing their ship. The captain announced that Germany had declared war on France, Great Britain, and Russia. When Great Britain and France raised their battle flags on the side of Russia, World War I, called the "War to End All Wars," began.

The captain of the Russian ship outran the German ships and docked at Alexandria, Egypt, where David and Ben-Zvi took a cargo ship for Jaffa. Once there, David went straight to the *Ahdut* offices. He told his fellow editors that the fate of the Jews in Palestine would depend upon Turkey. If Turkey sided with Germany against Russia, there would be reprisals from the Turkish government against Russian Jews in Palestine. Yet if Turkey sided with the Allies, including Russia, and won, then Russia, the most violent perpetrator of anti-Semitism, might overthrow the Ottoman Empire and set off pogroms in Palestine. Many Jews were so frightened they fled Palestine and went to live in neighboring Arab countries.

Ben-Gurion believed the Jews should support Turkey, as the Turks could not easily hurt people who backed them.

Most of the Po'alei Zion party agreed with him. David wrote editorials stressing the need for Jews to "Ottomanize" —become Turkish citizens. He and Ben-Zvi set up an office in the local rabbi's study to help the Jews fill out the necessary papers. Yet hardly anyone came. On October 31, Turkey entered the war allied with Germany. The Ottoman Empire immediately called for a *jihad,* a holy war, against the Jews. Turkish officials confiscated Jewish property, firearms, money, and food; banned signs written in Hebrew; and destroyed the Jewish Emergency Relief Committee's headquarters.

Now Jews fled Palestine in droves. Turkey's toughest military commander, Jamal Pasha, took charge of Palestine. Ben-Gurion suggested that writing editorials protesting Jamal's presence might encourage many Jews to stay in Palestine, for if there were no Jews in Palestine, there would be no Jewish state. The editors agreed. In response, Jamal sent *Ahdut* a written statement calling Jews "enemies of Turkey," and warning that anyone caught with a Zionist document would be executed. Only those Jews who swore to become Ottoman subjects would be spared. Then Jamal Pasha demanded that his statement be printed.

Fearing the flight of more Jews if they released Jamal's statement, *Ahdut*'s editors printed the statement, but never distributed that issue of *Ahdut.* Jamal discovered their trick and demanded that they distribute the journal. The editors of *Ahdut* had no choice. The Jewish response was surprising, however. The remaining Palestinian Jews, fearing arrest if they could not prove they were Turkish citizens, suddenly filled the "Ottomanization" office in the rabbi's study. David smiled in spite of the seriousness of the situation. The Turkish government had accomplished what he had been unable to—persuade Palestinian Jews to become Turkish citizens.

Turkish authorities then unexpectedly arrested *Ahdut*'s administrator because of the editorial against Jamal. The administrator lied to the police, saying that Ben-Zvi wrote the editorial, when actually one of the other editors wrote the protest. David was furious with the administrator and was concerned that Ben-Zvi would be arrested. In February 1915, David's fears came true. Yitzhak Ben-Zvi was arrested by the Turkish police. But so, too, was David Ben-Gurion.

They were charged with being anti-Ottoman for trying to establish a Jewish state in Palestine. Jamal ordered them deported as aliens, and "never again to set foot on Palestine soil."[8] David felt devastated by the thought of leaving his beloved Palestine. He and Ben-Zvi were put under house arrest in a Jaffa hotel until a ship arrived to take them out of the country. They decided to go to America, where they knew some members of the New York branch of the Po'alei Zion party.

Although David felt desolate, he tried to think positively about his exile. So far, his work to rebuild Israel involved unifying only Palestinian Jews. Maybe he needed to involve Jewish communities worldwide in Zionism. He and Ben-Zvi decided to establish a volunteer pioneer group in the United States that would emigrate to Palestine and help rebuild the barren land. The more Jews who emigrated, the faster the land could be redeveloped. And the faster the land was developed, the sooner the Jews could show Turkish rulers that Jews were capable of establishing and running an independent state.

On March 21, 1915, David Ben-Gurion and Yitzhak Ben-Zvi sat in a rowboat taking them from the port of Jaffa to an Italian ship anchored offshore. The two men were jostled by the motion of the sea as the tiny craft bounced over the waves. Ben-Gurion stared longingly back to shore. Nine years ago, he had fallen in love with this land when he had stood on the deck of another ship. His heart ached as he saw the shoreline grow smaller and smaller as the rowboat sailed farther and farther away from Palestine. "I'll be back one day," he swore.[9] His destiny commanded it.

THREE

★

A Zionist in America

David Ben-Gurion stared at the majestic lady with her arm held high, holding the torch of freedom in her hand. His heart skipped a beat as he and Yitzhak Ben-Zvi sailed past the Statue of Liberty. "Give me your tired, your poor, your huddled masses yearning to breathe free. . . ." David knew the inscription on the statue's pedestal. After being exiled from Palestine, he was now one of those tired, poor immigrants. Although he was homesick for Palestine, he was nevertheless filled with excitement over seeing the "Land of Golden Opportunity" for the first time. He and Ben-Zvi had even studied English while crossing the Atlantic.

In May 1915, while David Ben-Gurion was in the United States for the first time, Jewish leaders in Europe were trying to persuade Great Britain to let them form an army to help fight the Germans. Joseph Trumpeldor, a Jewish leader in Cairo, Egypt, was trying to get permission to organize what he called a "Jewish Mule Corps" to fight the Turks in Gallipoli. In London, Vladimir Jabotinsky, a noted poet and playwright, was trying to get permission to form a Jewish Legionnaire's army to aid the British.

In America, David's ship lumbered across New York Harbor and approached Ellis Island, the port of entry for immigrants. David's pulse quickened as he saw the immigration building, a drab structure that loomed ahead of him like a monster rising out of the sea. He opened his diary and wrote down his feelings: "I always dreamed of America, its vigorous, ultramodern life . . . in the most developed and most democratic country. We who want to build a new country in the desert . . . must see how exiles, persecuted in England, constructed a state so rich, with unequalled power."[1]

When the immigration authorities checked Ben-Gurion's and Ben-Zvi's papers and passed them through without any problems, David let out the breath he had been holding. Then they went to the Po'alei Zion headquarters, where Ben-Gurion told the members of his and Ben-Zvi's plan to get more American Jews to emigrate to Palestine. The head of the party offered to sponsor the two men on a tour of America's largest cities, where they could give speeches about Zionism.

Before he left for his tour, David talked to several young American Jews in New York. Their enthusiasm sparked another plan in his mind. He would try to enlist America's youth in the idea of joining a Jewish army. A unified defense force was one of Ben-Gurion's major goals for the new Israel. In a short time, he had organized the *Hehalutz*, a pioneer army of American Jewish youth.

While touring the United States, David tried to persuade other young Jews to join Hehalutz. During his travels, he was amazed by how Jews and Christians lived peacefully together in the same cities, many even in the same neighborhoods. He marveled at the freedom Americans enjoyed to express aloud their opinions about government policies. He thought how in Palestine, Turkish officials could arrest and exile a Jew just for making a minor complaint against the government.

On the other hand, David was shocked when he learned firsthand about segregation and the prejudice against blacks that existed in the United States. He had gone to a movie in Galveston, Texas, and was almost thrown out of the theater when he sat down in the black section. "Couldn't the sons of free, cultured, progressive, and democratic Americans learn a little humanity . . . ?" he asked.[2]

Ben-Gurion was equally disturbed by the apathetic response of Jewish audiences to his speeches asking them to move to Palestine and actively join the Zionist cause. When his tour ended, only sixty-three additional young people had joined Hehalutz. David was scheduled to give one more speech before returning to New York. Afterwards, he was surprised by that audience's enthusiastic reception. Many people in the audience even spoke up to challenge several of his ideas. David countered their arguments with such stimulating facts about Zionism and the need for the Hehalutz that his challengers were left speechless. The news of David's speaking abilities spread, and people from other states asked him to give lectures in their cities. Audiences particularly wanted to hear David's ruthless, often sarcastic, counterattacks against doubting anti-Zionists.

At a rally in Minnesota, Ben-Gurion debated one anti-Zionist with particular venom. Afterwards, for some strange reason, David was thought of as a hero. Yet not all American Zionists looked up to him as a modern-day Messiah. At a rally in Milwaukee, Wisconsin, a bright-eyed young woman named Goldie Mabovich said she was bored. In the future, Ben-Gurion would know Goldie quite well, for she was about to emigrate to Palestine, where one day, under her new Hebrew name Golda Meir, she would be elected the only female prime minister Israel has ever had.

In June 1915, David spoke at a Zionist rally in New

York City. Another speaker that evening was Louis D. Brandeis, a lawyer who eventually became a Supreme Court Justice. Brandeis talked about Zionism's effect on American Jews: "It seeks to establish in Palestine for such Jews as choose to go and remain there . . . a legally secured home, where they . . . may expect ultimately to constitute a majority of the population, and may look forward to what we should call home rule."[3]

Ben-Gurion's speeches in the United States influenced Zionists in other countries to work toward getting Jews living in their cities to join the Zionist cause. Zionism received even more publicity when David's and Ben-Zvi's book collaboration about Jewish life in the Pale of Settlement in Poland, titled *Yizkor*, meaning "Remembrance," was listed on the international best-sellers' list. Ben-Zvi was in Washington, D.C., at the time, and David relished having the spotlight all to himself. He was besieged with lecture invitations, and the name David Ben-Gurion became known all over the United States.

Yet for all his successes, David was lonely. He yearned to see Rachel and he wrote her a letter pleading for her to come to America. Rachel did not reply. David fell into depression and refused to go out with friends. One night, in the summer of 1916, a friend finally persuaded him to attend a dinner party. There, he met Paula Munweiss, an immigrant from Minsk, Russia, who worked as a nurse in a New York City clinic. David liked Paula and found it easy to talk to her.

Paula and David started seeing each other regularly. Often Paula packed a lunch, and they rented a rowboat at Coney Island for a day of picnicking. While they ate, David found himself telling Paula more about his life and his dream than he had ever told anyone. The more he was with Paula the more he liked her. He knew he would never experience the same kind of intense love with Paula that he had had with Rachel, but he believed a less passionate relationship would allow him time to pursue his dream without feeling guilty for neglecting the woman he loved.

Paula fell deeply in love with the shy, intelligent young man from Plonsk. She encouraged him in his efforts to achieve his dream, and attempted to learn more about Zionism.

"I loved him because he was full of life," she once said. "And I saw in him that he had something great. Being head of a movement or state had nothing to do with it—he would be great anyway."[4]

During this time Ben-Gurion and Ben-Zvi started a new book collaboration, titled *Eretz Israel: The Land of Our Fathers*. The book described the history of Palestine in a modern way which David hoped would entice more young Jews into emigrating to Palestine. Paula helped David do research for the book, while also making sure he ate nourishing meals and got enough rest.

On November 2, 1917, David's spirits soared when he read a letter published in a British newspaper. The British foreign minister, Arthur Balfour, had written to Lord Rothschild, the philanthropist who had helped Jews emigrate to Palestine, that, "His Majesty's Government view with favour the establishment in Palestine of a national home for the Jewish People, and will use their best endeavours to facilitate the achievement of this object. . . ."[5]

Although this message, known as the "Balfour Declaration," was careful not to specify a home-*land*, Balfour's words laid the foundation for the establishment of the State of Israel. Ben-Gurion had high hopes that he was moving closer to accomplishing his dream.

In April 1917, the United States entered World War I on the side of Great Britain, and Ben-Gurion stopped his attempts to expand the Hehalutz into a military force that would fight with Turkey against the British. With Great Britain and America now allies, Ben-Gurion believed fighting the British would mean declaring war on the United States, a strong Zionist supporter.

On December 15, 1917, David Ben-Gurion and Paula Munweiss were married in a civil ceremony at City Hall in New York City, and they moved into an apartment in Brooklyn. The newlyweds had only a short time together, as in February 1918, when Paula was expecting their first child, the British agreed to let Vladimir Jabotinsky form his Jewish Legion. Almost immediately, legion recruiting offices opened in the United States, and David Ben-Gurion was one of the first in line.

In May, David Ben-Gurion and Yitzhak Ben-Zvi, who had also joined the legion, were assigned to the Forty-second Battalion of the Royal Fusiliers and shipped to a military base north of Cairo. By the time they arrived, however, the war was ending and neither man had a chance to fight. Nevertheless, David was a dedicated soldier, and soon he was promoted to the rank of corporal.

On September 19, 1918, the last Turkish stronghold in Palestine fell to the British. Six weeks later World War I ended, and along with it, four hundred years of Turkish rule in Palestine. Ben-Gurion and Ben-Zvi were sweltering in a tent in the Egyptian desert at the time, waiting to be demobilized from their unit. David's boredom was interrupted by a cable from the United States that Paula had delivered a baby girl. The child was named Geula, meaning "liberation." David was overjoyed about the birth, but disappointed that he could not be in New York to hold his first child.

Left with little to do until he was discharged, David spent his days talking to other legionnaires about his future plans for Palestine. One of these men was thirty-two-year-old Berl Katzenelson. Berl was not affiliated with the Zionist party, and preferred to lead his own group of workers. For the rest of David's life, Berl Katzenelson would have a calming influence on David's frequent impulsive, rash behavior. Ben-Gurion would turn to Katzenelson whenever he needed advice or someone to listen to his plans for the new Israel. He came to love Berl as a brother.

Finally David's legionnaire unit was demobilized, and he, Katzenelson, and Ben-Zvi went to Jaffa to attend a Po'alei Zion meeting. They were horrified at how the war had demolished the city. The inhabitants now lived in worse poverty than when David first arrived in Palestine. Almost everyone suffered from disease and starvation, while crops rotted in the fields. Most horrendous of all were the Jews whom the Turks had put in jail. When the Turks fled Jaffa, they left these Jews locked up. Most of these Jews had died, but the few who survived were found barely conscious.

While he was in Jaffa, David learned that Rachel was now living with her husband and children outside Tel Aviv. He went to visit her and ended up staying as a guest in her home. Rachel showed David the letters his sister Zippora had written to her from Poland. He was moved by Rachel's consideration. Even though the war had ended, David had not heard from his family. He was glad to learn they were safe. David was happy being with Rachel. He still loved her in spite of his marriage and newborn daughter.

With the war over, Ben-Gurion resumed his efforts to unite workers into a political labor party. He persuaded members of the Po'alei Zion to merge with other labor groups. The Hapoel Hatzair party, the Po'alei Zion's biggest rival, refused to merge. David was infuriated that their resistance might sabotage his entire strategy to form a powerful Jewish labor-political movement, one that would help establish the Jewish state.

In late February 1919, Berl Katzenelson agreed to merge his independent labor group with the Po'alei Zion party, and a labor union, called the *Ahdut HaAvodah*,

While in America to promote the international goals of Zionism, Ben-Gurion met and married Paula Munweiss in 1916.

"Union of Labor," was created. Workers from all stations in life rejoiced in the hope that now they would have their Jewish state.

Ben-Gurion realized, however, that although the Balfour Declaration promised the Jews a home, it did not promise them land on which they could build this home. He suggested interpreting the declaration as if it had spelled out "homeland in Palestine." He reasoned that the Arabs were interpreting the declaration their own way, by blaming the British for reneging on their promise to give *them* control over Palestine once the Turks were ousted from the Middle East. The Arabs accused the Jews of taking over their land.

In November 1919, Ben-Gurion felt the time was right to send for Paula and his daughter, Geula. When they arrived, David was enthralled with his daughter. He showed Geula a gentleness that others, including Paula, did not know he possessed.

The Ben-Gurions rented a small apartment in the primitive village of Tel Aviv. Paula proved herself a good sport for someone who had never gone without modern conveniences. She quickly accustomed herself to using an outdoor bathroom, and to bathing, washing clothes, and scrubbing dishes all in the same tin tub. Paula's hardest adjustment was getting used to David's long absences. She decided to make the best of their time together. When David arrived home late at night, exhausted from attending labor party meetings all day, Paula made sure that hot water filled the tub and a nourishing meal was on the table.

Meanwhile, the atmosphere in the King David Hotel, which housed the British Mandate offices, grew thick with apprehension that the Arabs would make good their threat to retaliate against the British for giving the Jews "their land." Therefore, even before the ink was dry on the Balfour Declaration, the British had started to change its provisions.

Early in 1920, the Arabs drove a further wedge between Great Britain and the Jews. The League of Nations, formed after World War I, had put Syria and Lebanon under a French Mandate. The Bedouins feared the French would try to claim their land in the northern Galilee. On March 1, they attacked French troops in the Galilee, including two Jewish villages they mistakenly believed were French. In the mayhem, Joseph Trumpeldor, creator of the Jewish Mule Corps, and the leader of Tel Hai, one of the Jewish villages, was killed. Shortly afterward, the Jews formed an underground army named the *Haganah*, meaning "Defense," to defend Jewish lives and property. The Haganah was headed by Vladimir Jabotinsky, the former commander of the Jewish Legion.

In Jerusalem, Mufti (Moslem leader) Haj Amin el-Husseini had kept a watchful eye on the Tel Hai massacre. When he realized the British had done nothing to stop the attack, el-Husseini interpreted the British inaction as a green light to continue the slaughter of Jews begun by the Bedouin. Haj Amin decided to launch his first attack against the sacred city of Jerusalem, the soul of Zionism. El-Husseini stroked his red beard and considered how to carry off the attack. The Jewish holiday Passover was coming up, and an Arab religious holiday would occur at the same time. A group of Arabs walking down a Jewish street on their way to worship would not attract undue attention from the Jews, at least not until the Arabs were told the Jews planned to seize the Moslem's holy places. Then the Arab worshippers would turn into a bloodthirsty mob.

FOUR

★

The Turbulent Twenties

On Passover morning, in April 1920, David Ben-Gurion sat in Yitzhak Ben-Zvi's kitchen having breakfast with Ben-Zvi and his new wife, Rachel Yanait. While David sipped tea and ate matzoh, the unleavened bread eaten during Passover, he suddenly heard a thunderous noise outside. He rushed to the window and saw a mob running down the street, their boots stirring up the dust. At that moment, Rachel's father burst into the house shouting that Arabs were beating up Jews in the Old City of Jerusalem, and the British had sealed off the entrance to the Old City, blocking efforts to rescue Jews trapped inside.

Ben-Gurion turned pale. He and Ben-Zvi ran to the Old City, determined to save the Jews. By the time they arrived, however, the riot was over. British officials charged Vladimir Jabotinsky and twenty Haganah men with "the evil intent of bringing about rapine, pillage, devastation of country, and homicide, etc.,"[1] and sentenced them to several years of hard labor. Even though the British high commissioner, Sir Herbert Samuel, sent to Palestine to enforce the

Balfour Declaration, gave the Haganah men amnesty three months later, the Arab riot proved to the Jews what David Ben-Gurion had been telling them for a long time. If they wanted to have the Jewish homeland that the Balfour Declaration had promised, they would have to unite.

A few days after the riot, 77 percent of Palestinian Jews crowded the polls and voted for an Elected Assembly, the first Jewish "parliament" ever formed. The new labor union, Ahdut HaAvodah, received a one-third majority, making it the largest faction in the Elected Assembly. Although Great Britain did not allow the parliament to meet, Ben-Gurion felt hopeful. For once, his dream seemed to be moving forward without delays.

A calm settled over the Middle East. Palestinian Arabs who had previously lived, with their animals, in mud houses without sanitation, and Arab farmers who, ignorant of modern methods, never produced a decent crop, started to copy the Jewish life-style. The Arabs built clean houses with outside sheds for their animals; switched to modern irrigation methods; brought their children to Jewish clinics to be treated for diseases; and learned about personal hygiene from Jewish nurses. Jewish textile factories and power plants provided jobs for these Arabs, and, as a result, close to thirty thousand Arabs moved to Palestine from Syria, Transjordan, and Iraq.

Palestinian Arabs and Jews might have continued living in peace together if the Arab landowners outside Palestine had not become angry when Arab laborers suddenly demanded higher wages and better living conditions. Taking advantage of strong Moslem religious beliefs, the landowners fought back by telling Arab workers that the Jews were pagans. The peasants rioted in Jerusalem and the Upper Galilee. Many Jews were killed before the British Mandate government stopped the massacres.

Great Britain, fearing that the uprisings would hurt British relations with Arab rulers in neighboring countries, limited new Jewish immigration into Palestine. To make matters worse, the British high commissioner, himself a

Jew, tried to show impartiality by promoting Amin el-Husseini, the main instigator of the riots, to the position of grand mufti, thereby making him the chief Moslem religious leader for life. In addition, the British forbade Jews from living in Transjordan, the plateau east of the Jordan River, and made Prince Abdullah the ruler there as a reward for his help during World War I.

Ben-Gurion was enraged. Originally this territory had been designated part of the Jewish homeland. Adding to his troubles, disagreements plagued the Zionist movement itself. One group of Zionists agreed with Chaim Weizmann, a renowned Jewish chemist, and a strong admirer of the British, who believed the Jews should trust Great Britain to honor the Balfour Declaration. Another Zionist faction refused to accept Ben-Gurion's socialist form of government for the Jewish state. David wanted to mediate a compromise between the two factions, but in June 1920 the Ahdut HaAvodah labor union sent him to London for the first World Zionist Congress since 1913.

Paula and Geula went with him. Paula was delighted to stay in a hotel, especially since she was expecting their second child. At the Zionist conference, Ben-Gurion pressed the British to follow through on the Balfour Declaration, and in addition asked for more financial backing to rebuild Palestine. He stuck to his belief that what Palestine needed most was money to build settlements, industries, and roads. In response, Chaim Weizmann charged the *Yishuv* with impulsiveness in its demand that Great Britain enforce the Balfour Declaration immediately.

Ben-Gurion sat silently fuming. When his turn came to speak, he asked why, if the pioneers of Israel could make great sacrifices, the World Zionist Organization could not make a few themselves? After all, every Jew present had the same goal—the establishment of a national homeland. Weizmann countered by vehemently putting down Ben-Gurion's ideas. However, Weizmann's criticisms were couched in such eloquent language that many attendees, although moved by Ben-Gurion's pleas, nevertheless voted against him. Weizmann's acid tone would become commonplace as a bitter power struggle erupted between Jewish farmers and Zionists.

On September 28, 1920, Paula gave birth to a baby boy. His parents named him Amos, after the prophet who promised the Israelites they would return to their land. Because of minor medical complications, Paula had to remain in the hospital a while after Amos was released. David took care of the children, and he was surprised at how well he managed. Holding a crying Geula while running to give Amos his noon bottle became as routine to David as giving Zionist speeches. "I can't leave the house," he wrote his father, "and I have learned what raising children means."[2]

By March 1921, Ben-Gurion had spent all the money the HaAvodah had given him for his time in London. He sent Paula and the children to Plonsk to stay with his father while he looked for a job. Eventually the Po'alei Zion party in Vienna hired him to work in their office. Two months later, Communist and moderate Zionists physically fought each other in Jaffa. However, the report that spread said the Jews had attacked the Arabs. Moslem gangs went on a rampage, beating up every Jew they could find, then stabbing them to death.

The British high commissioner blamed the Jews. As punishment, he stopped all Jewish immigration into Palestine, a blatant violation of the Balfour Declaration. British officials ignored Ben-Gurion's complaints that they were reneging on their promise. Feeling helpless and drained of energy from all the bickering, and missing Paula and the children, David decided to take a vacation in Plonsk. He had not seen his immediate family in fourteen years. Ben-Gurion arrived in Plonsk in July 1921. When he saw his father, happiness overwhelmed him.

In December, Ben-Gurion was still in Plonsk when he received a message from Palestine that his efforts to create a labor union "army" had come true. Jewish workers from all areas of employment had united to form one single organization, called the *Histadrut*, from the Hebrew words

A powerful public speaker, Ben-Gurion addresses an audience in 1924 at the Labor Building in Jerusalem. He was then secretary of the Histadrut (the General Federation of Hebrew Workers).

meaning "the General Federation of Hebrew Workers in *Eretz Yisrael.*" Eager to be making the decisions for the new organization, Ben-Gurion left Paula and the children in Plonsk, where they would be safe from rioting Arabs, and returned to Palestine.

The Histadrut elected David secretary of the party. Under his direction, the Histadrut established departments to handle all aspects of running a state, including education, agriculture, commerce, transportation, and defense, with the Haganah becoming the military branch of the Histadrut.

By the mid-1920s, the Fourth Aliyah had brought close to thirty-five thousand Jewish immigrants into Palestine. They were fleeing from a new wave of pogroms in Eastern Europe, and many chose Palestine because no other country would take them in. The United States had passed the Immigration Act of 1924, which severely limited the number of Eastern European immigrants allowed into America.

In Palestine, the new immigrants assimilated into the Jewish life-style, especially by joining political parties. The Histadrut's membership swelled. In February 1922, Ben-Gurion moved Histadrut's headquarters from Tel Aviv to Jerusalem, the traditional capital of Palestine. During this time, he shared a squalid one-room apartment with a colleague. They had only one bed—a hard board propped on two oil cans—which the two men took turns sleeping on. While David Ben-Gurion lived in modest suroundings, many of the wealthier Jewish immigrants had escaped with their life savings. They settled in Haifa, Jerusalem, the outskirts of Jaffa, and Tel Aviv, which became an all-Jewish city. Stucco houses replaced dilapidated shanties, and tall buildings, factories, and warehouses sprang up out of the sand. Tel Aviv blossomed into a bustling, crowded metropolis.

Ben-Gurion was troubled by the situation in Tel Aviv. As prices soared and salaries dwindled, Histadrut offices were crowded with unemployed Jews. Big-city profits were soon exhausted, and the Jewish economy plummeted. Many firms declared bankruptcy. A typhoid epidemic struck the final blow to the rich urban population, and many fled Palestine. Ben-Gurion tried to instill hope into the Jews who remained. Nevertheless, from the middle to late 1920s, thousands of Jews left Palestine at the same time that thousands more entered.

When David wanted to escape the problems connected with developing a country, he visited Rachel. He could barely tolerate her husband, but forced himself to stay on friendly terms with him in order to spend time with Rachel. David felt comfortable enough with Rachel to tell her his feelings about Palestinian politics without letting his love for her sidetrack him from his dream. Their love for each other had endured over the years, if not their freedom to act upon their love.

At the same time, David missed Paula and his children, and felt guilty for leaving them so long with his father. He abruptly sent for them. Then he happily prepared for his family's homecoming by getting the sewing machine repaired, and buying chairs, a stove, a broom, and a pail. Minutes before their train was due, David had his shoes shined. Once his family was settled, Ben-Gurion resumed his push for the removal of immigration restrictions against Jews, and for financial aid for the Histadrut. David was so poor himself that he started buying a one-way ticket to European Zionist meetings, then wiring his friends in Palestine to send him the return fare if they ever wanted to see him again.

When the European Zionists refused to give any money to Histadrut, Ben-Gurion grew desperate. He turned to an unlikely source for a Jew—the Russians. He believed that out of three million Jews living in Russia, some of them had to be wealthy. If he were on friendly terms with the Russians, perhaps they would let more Jews emigrate to Palestine. By a lucky coincidence, the Soviet government had just sent Ben-Gurion an invitation to lead the Histadrut delegation at Moscow's International Agricultural Exhibition that was scheduled to open in the summer of 1923.

In Moscow, many Soviet Jews visited the Histadrut exhibition, even though they could be arrested merely for entering the exhibition hall itself. Jewish Communists, however, were adamantly opposed to Zionism and tried to get the Histadrut exhibit barred. Failing that, they wrote an article declaring that Histadrut produce was grown by exploited Arabs. Ben-Gurion was stunned to hear Jews speak against Zionism.

He was about to close the exhibit, when a Zionist scout leader whispered something in his ear. David followed him to a small, dark apartment. Inside were more scouts. They greeted Ben-Gurion in Hebrew, and tears sprang to his eyes. The scouts asked David what Palestine was like, and he told them about his dream.

Suddenly heavy boots clomped outside the door. "The Russian secret police!" one scout hissed. Two others shoved a Russian cap over David's head and hustled him out a back entrance. "Shalom," Ben-Gurion whispered, then hurried back to the exhibition. As he ran, one of the scouts exclaimed, "What a man!" The word spread about Ben-Gurion's heroic escape from the Russian secret police, along with his need for more Jews in Palestine. Soon Jewish youths were sneaking across borders and making their way to the Holy Land.

After Ben-Gurion's experiences in Moscow, he opposed communism even more. When the Russian dictator Lenin died in 1924, he was succeeded by Joseph Stalin, a strong anti-Semite. David expelled all Jewish Communists from the Histadrut and forced employers not to hire them. Many Zionist far-leftists, members of Israel Shochat's Hapoel Hatzair party, opposed Ben-Gurion's anti-Communist policies. Shochat had even asked the Russians to support a Communist-Zionist state. The Histadrut gave Shochat an ultimatum: Give up your weapons or leave Palestine. Shochat remained, although many of his followers went to Russia, where Stalin immediately had them executed.

FIVE

★

The Prophet Emerges

The multiple problems of trying to establish peace with the Arabs, unify leftist and rightist Zionists, and convince the British to enforce the Balfour Declaration took almost all of Ben-Gurion's time. He had little time to spend with his family. David was out of town so much his family joked that he pretended he did not recognize his children when he came home. One time he boarded a bus, sat down next to a boy whom he thought was Amos, and immediately started scolding him for something Amos had done. Not until the boy got off the bus did Ben-Gurion realize the boy was not Amos. When he told Paula about his mistake, she was so mortified she made David climb on the roof and yell to the children, "Dinner! Dinner!" so they would recognize their father's voice, and the neighbors would think he cared about them.

Yet for all his inattention, his children adored him. To them, David Ben-Gurion was not a public figure, but rather "Oppu" (Papa), the man whose pockets were filled with treats whenever he walked in the door. Amos never had a birthday party because David was never home to celebrate with him. Yet Ben-Gurion always remembered the childrens' birthdays, and sent them presents.

Often David would be out of town during Hanukkah, the Jewish festival of lights, in which Jewish children receive one present each night for eight nights. No matter where he was, Ben-Gurion never forgot to send his children presents. A custom of Hanukkah is to give children a small amount of money, called *Hanukkah Gelt.* David would always say he gave each child an amount equal to every year of his or her life. Then he would add, "But those under seven will get an extra five piasters."[1] This was his way of making the youngest child feel as important as the oldest.

In 1925, Paula gave birth to their third child, a girl. They named the baby Renana, meaning "exultation." Although David loved Geula and Amos, he felt a special attachment to Renana from the minute he laid eyes upon her. Every day he wrote down her height and weight. When she lost her first baby tooth, David celebrated as if the occasion were a national event.

Even though David was seldom around his children, he possessed an uncanny ability to parent them. Renana once threw a temper tantrum, complaining that Amos had more chocolate than she did. Ben-Gurion furrowed his bushy brows. "You want more chocolate?" he asked. "*Say* that you want more—not that Amos gets more than you have."[2] He was trying to teach Renana that what another person has is not a yardstick to measure your own needs.

Another time Amos was angry at Geula and Renana and hit them. Paula sent Amos to be spanked by his father, who was in the living room at the time. When Amos walked in, Ben-Gurion looked up at his son and said, "Amos, when I am old, the one thing I'll regret is that I didn't pay enough attention to you in your early life. But I have a mission to perform and I cannot divide my attention. So please, Amos, try to reduce the burden that I shall feel when I am old."[3]

Amos was deeply moved. His father had never spoken to him in such an open, emotional way before. "Don't worry, Father," Amos said. "I'll find my way. You go ahead with your mission."[4]

In July 1925, David finally convinced his father to move to Palestine. When Avigdor saw David, he was shocked at how much his son had changed since he last saw him four years earlier. David's hair was streaked with gray, and he had put on weight. He looked much older than his thirty-nine years.

Avigdor moved into a house with David's sister Zippora and her children, and David found him a job working as an accountant for the Histadrut construction firm. A short time later, David's sister Rivka's husband died, and she decided to emigrate to Palestine. Then David's brothers Michael and Avraham arrived with their families. Soon all of Ben-Gurion's relatives were living in Palestine. Yet he had little time to spend with them, especially since Paula kept the number of David's visitors to a minimum. She felt that if David had any free time, he was going to spend it with her and their children.

After helping his family get settled, Ben-Gurion threw himself into his work. He traveled from country to country raising money for the Histadrut. By the late 1920s the labor union's treasury was filled with enough funds to help develop the Jewish economy, and Ben-Gurion resumed his push for a united labor political party. Berl Katzenelson helped by writing editorials in the newspaper he created for the labor party, the Ahdut HaAvodah. He proposed a merger between the Hapoel Hatzair party and the Ahdut HaAvodah. In 1926, the two parties held a referendum and voted to merge, with the final signing of the merger to be held when all their differences were settled.

Meanwhile, the Arabs started complaining to the British again about the Jewish presence in Palestine. After the early 1920 Arab riots, both Jews and Arabs had lived in relative peace for a while. The Jewish population in Palestine rose to 162,000, while the Arab population increased to 800,000, mainly as a result of Jewish instruction in health and living conditions. Under the British high commissioner's rule, the British workers built a network of roads to develop transportation and trade. British officials even worked with the Jews to fight malaria, drain swamps, build schools, and put hospitals and health services in almost every village.

Toward the end of the decade, however, the mufti encouraged discontent among Arab workers by blaming the increased number of Jews in Palestine for taking away Arab jobs. In addition, the mufti accused the British of keeping Arabs from holding offices in the Palestinian government.

In July 1929, the World Zionist Congress voted to establish the Jewish Agency for Palestine to work with British officials in governing the Jews in Palestine. The agency would also ask Jews for donations to rebuild the land in Palestine. Arab workers perceived the agency's negotiations with the British as the final Jewish threat to their existence in Palestine. The morning after the agency was formed, an Arab mob rioted in the Old City of Jerusalem. Arab workers attacked Jews who were in the middle of saying prayers at the Western Wall, and massacred the residents of Jewish communities in the ancient cities of Safed, Haifa, and Hebron. Only the Jewish settlements guarded by the Haganah were prepared to defend themselves, and the Arabs withdrew from these villages.

The riot lasted several days before the British finally stopped the killings. Great Britain's hesitation was motivated by the desire to remain on friendly terms with the Arabs. The British depended upon Arabs in Iraq and Saudi Arabia to protect British oil deposits there. Moreover, in its efforts to appease the Arabs, the British Mandate government limited land sales to Jews and further restricted Jewish immigration into Palestine. Ben-Gurion demanded that these restrictions be removed, as they were illegal according to the British Mandate. Great Britain refused.

Because there was no further recourse open to him, Ben-Gurion turned his attention to settling the remaining differences between the Hapoel Hatzair party and the HaAvodat, so the two labor parties could finalize their merger. In January 1930, the contracts were signed, and a new political labor party was declared, named *Mapai*, from the Hebrew initials for "Eretz Israel Workers' party." Although Ben-Gurion was hailed as a hero, he could not give his whole heart over to the rejoicing that followed. A sense of foreboding washed over him that the Jews were going to endure much more oppression before they would have their Jewish homeland.

As David Ben-Gurion climbed ever higher toward becoming the leader of Zionism, he kept his eyes on two Zionists—Vladimir Jabotinsky and Chaim Weizmann, president of the World Zionist Organization. When Jabotinsky quit the Histadrut in the early 1920s, he formed a right-wing Zionist party, called the Revisionists, who believed in a Jewish state at any cost. Jabotinsky and his Revisionists incited an Arab riot in 1929 when they demonstrated at the Western Wall to protest an Arab newspaper article claiming that Jews only pretended to pray at the wall, while in reality they were planning to destroy the nearby Mosque of Omar. The Jews would then rebuild the temple that had stood on that spot over two thousand years ago.

Ben-Gurion, who believed in using restraint when defending Jews against Arab attacks, feared that Jabotinsky's violent tactics might jeopardize chances of the British ever putting the Balfour Declaration into effect. At the same time, he was growing frustrated with Chaim Weizmann dragging his feet whenever he was supposed to ask the British for concessions for the Jews. In addition, Weizmann had insisted that the British could be trusted; and then Lord Passfield, the British colonial secretary, had delivered his "White Paper" (a proclamation in a white binding), limiting Jewish immigration and land purchases in Palestine.

Weizmann was now hesitating to pressure the British into rescinding these Jewish restrictions. Ben-Gurion believed Weizmann's passiveness was delaying the establishment of a Jewish state, and he decided to force Weizmann's "early retirement" and take over the presidency of the World Zionist Organization himself. Then Ben-Gurion would be chairman of the largest political organization in Palestine, giving him the necessary power to push through resolutions to establish the new Israel in the fastest way possible. To accomplish this feat, Ben-Gurion would have to persuade more Jews to join Mapai, so the party would have more delegates than Weizmann at the 1933 World Zionist Congress. Then Weizmann would be forced to step down.

Weizmann, aware that his popularity was fading, pleaded with his British friends to get rid of the White Paper. Great Britain relented, and in February 1931, Prime Minister Ramsay MacDonald partly rescinded the White Paper by placing fewer restrictions on Jewish immigration and land purchases. Nevertheless, when the 1931 World Zionist Congress convened, Weizmann was defeated for reelection by a moderate Zionist named Nahum Sokolow. However, since Weizmann would be Sokolow's adviser, he would still run the World Zionist Organization from the sidelines.

During the congress, Prime Minister MacDonald told Ben-Gurion privately that he might be willing to set up a Jewish-Arab legislative assembly on the basis of parity, or equal representation, even though the Arabs outnumbered the Jews. A surge of hope swelled inside Ben-Gurion. A legislative assembly meant that he could claim Palestine as the Jewish state as soon as enough immigrants arrived to give the Jews a majority in Palestine.

Meanwhile, Vladimir Jabotinsky's proposals at the congress were not accepted, and he stormed out. Ben-Gurion hoped he would never return. The congress formed a five-man Zionist Executive Committee, and two men were chosen from Mapai. Now Ben-Gurion felt even more certain that Mapai would take over the World Zionist Organization. All he needed was for Mapai to win a majority of labor delegates to the next World Zionist Congress to be held in August 1933. For the next two years Ben-Gurion's main occupation was campaigning for Mapai delegates.

By April 1933, David was so deeply immersed in this campaign that he did not take time off to check into recent Jewish immigrants' reports about the violent anti-Semitic oppression that was occurring in Eastern Europe. He argued that letting Eastern European Jews emigrate to Palestine ahead of Jews from other countries was unfair. Ben-Gurion believed, as did most world leaders of the time, that Adolf Hitler's harassment of German Jews was merely another anti-Semitic storm that would soon blow over. Unfortunately, this complacent attitude gave Hitler, now chancellor of Germany, time to transform his anti-Semitic oppression into what was to become a Holocaust.

In the meantime, a mysterious murder case solved Ben-Gurion's problem of getting more Mapai delegates for the 1933 World Zionist Congress. Chaim Arlosoff, sent by the Jewish Agency to Berlin to negotiate a transfer of German Jews to Palestine, was murdered on a deserted Tel Aviv beach shortly after his return. A Revisionist named Avraham Stavsky was found guilty of the crime and sentenced to hang. Yet for unknown reasons, his sentence was revoked and the murderer was never found. The controversial case caused many Palestinian Jews to turn against the Revisionist philosophy of violence, and to vote for Mapai delegates to the World Zionist Congress.

As a result, when the Eighteenth World Zionist Congress opened in Prague, Czechoslovakia, on August 25, 1933, the Mapai party was represented by a majority of delegates. The attendees almost shattered the windows with their cheers for Ben-Gurion. He found it hard to believe that twenty-seven years ago, clad in a tattered Russian shirt and sandals, he had walked to his first Po'alei Zion conference in Jaffa, only to be scorned for such a revolutionary idea as a Jewish state. During the congress, Ben-Gurion was appointed to the Jewish Agency Executive.

His popularity soared, and two years later, David was elected the first Palestinian chairman of the executive, making him the "prime minister" of an unrecognized Jewish government in Palestine, and giving him control over the policies for building a Jewish homeland. Thus David Ben-Gurion became the person who wielded more power than any other Zionist in the world.

As chairman, he lived for several months each year in London, the home base of the Zionist Executive Committee. Living expenses were higher in London than in Palestine, and he now had to pay for two living places. Paula helped support the family by renting part of their house in Tel Aviv to tourists and by resuming her former occupation as a nurse.

While Paula learned how to budget, Ben-Gurion learned he had made a dreadful mistake by ignoring reports about a new wave of anti-Semitism in Eastern Europe. At a Histadrut meeting, he prophesied that Hitler would not stop killing Jews when he annihilated Germany's Jews, but would "wage a war of vengeance against France, Poland, Czechoslovakia, and other countries where a Jewish population is to be found. . . . Perhaps only four or five years . . . stand between us and that awful day. . . . We must double our numbers, for the size of the Jewish community then may determine our fate in that decisive hour."[5]

Ben-Gurion frantically sought ways to get German Jews into Palestine. Since Great Britain granted visas only to immigrants with jobs waiting for them in Palestine, Ben-Gurion called for the creation of every job imaginable, from ditchdiggers to botanists. He persuaded newspaper reporters to write editorials favoring Jewish immigration.

At the 1935 World Zionist Congress, Ben-Gurion, dressed in his usual rumpled gray suit and white shirt

open at the collar, moved that Chaim Weizmann resume the presidency of the World Zionist Organization, believing that Weizmann possessed the distinction necessary to make a good Zionist ambassador. Weizmann accepted.

Meanwhile, in 1935 Adolf Hitler had become "Fuhrer." As leader of Germany, Hitler was now free to make Germany, and then the world, *Judenrein,* meaning "Jew-free." Hitler's armies stormed across Europe, later stretching into Czechoslovakia, and then in 1939 into Poland, where three million Jews remained trapped, unable to get visas from Great Britain to go to Palestine. And almost no one, not even David Ben-Gurion, the "Prophet of Israel," as he had come to be called, could foresee the horrendous nightmare that lay ahead for Europe's Jews.

Ben-Gurion answers questions from journalists in his new role as the Chairman of the Jewish Agency Executive in 1936.

SIX

★

Let My People Go

While Ben-Gurion took steps to hasten the creation of a Jewish state, Adolf Hitler took his first step to rid Germany of its Jews. In 1935 he enacted the "Nuremberg Laws," which revoked the citizenship of Jews and forbade them to marry non-Jews, apply for jobs, or attend universities. In addition, Jews had to wear armbands with the Star of David to identify them as Jews.

Ben-Gurion worked frantically to get German Jews into Palestine. His method was to enlist as many new members as possible into Mapai, on the premise that a large Jewish labor party could wield enough power to force Great Britain to allow all Jewish immigrants into Palestine. At the same time, Ben-Gurion believed a large Jewish political organization would be in a better position to negotiate a truce with the Arabs. Many times in the past, he had offered to meet with Arab leaders to negotiate a peace settlement between Moslems and Jews. Yet each time, the two peoples reached an impasse on one issue—whether there should be a Jewish or an Arab majority in Palestine.

In April 1936, the Arabs formed a Supreme Arab Committee. One of its first acts was to ban all land sales to Jews, and to call for a workers' strike until Great Britain stopped all Jewish immigration into Palestine and formed an Arab majority government. Then, to emphasize their demands, the Arabs went on a rampage, knifing and shooting Jews and Britons alike.

Ben-Gurion ordered the Haganah, which had become Israel's national army, to fight back, but cautioned them to use their weapons only for defense. He did not want to antagonize the British, as their support was critical for establishing the Jewish state. Ben-Gurion knew he could trust the Haganah to follow his orders, but he felt helpless to control the Revisionist party's military branch, the *Irgun Zvai Leumi*, led by Vladimir Jabotinsky. The Irgun hurled bombs into British government buildings and Arab shops, kidnapped British soldiers, and assassinated public figures. Their actions infuriated Ben-Gurion, who believed the Irgun was damaging the reputation of the Jewish national army. For the rest of his life, Ben-Gurion would attack anyone who slurred the name of "his soldiers."

In the meantime, the Arab strike backfired, as the British government allowed more Jewish immigrants into Palestine to fill jobs vacated by the Arabs. In addition, when Arab dockworkers in Jaffa joined the strike, the Jews built another dock in Tel Aviv and employed Jewish immigrants as stevedores. The Arabs finally realized what was happening and attacked the Jews with renewed force, threatening to continue the onslaught until Great Britain met their demands.

Ben-Gurion pleaded with British officials not to give in. This time, the British, having witnessed Arab aggression toward Britons, in contrast to the Haganah's restraint, allowed Jewish immigration into Palestine to continue. The British decision saved the lives of many European Jews from Hitler's "final solution." The Mandate government even supplied Haganah soldiers with arms, and sent more British troops to help keep order in Palestine.

Moreover, some of the British soldiers believed the Jews had a right to defend themselves. One in particular was Captain Charles Orde Wingate. At Ben-Gurion's request, Wingate took four hundred Jews and two hundred British volunteers into the Jerusalem hills and trained the Jews to fight using the commando tactics of guerrilla warfare. The Jews turned into "Special Night Squads" of the Haganah, and became known as "Wingate's Raiders." In turn, the "Raiders" taught Jewish farmers and laborers Wingate's fighting tactics.

In November 1936, the Arabs called off their strike and stopped the Jewish raids. Nevertheless, the British realized the Mandate was not working. Great Britain sent a new Royal High Commission to Palestine, led by Lord Earl Peel, to investigate the Arab-Jewish conflict. The Peel Commission recommended dividing Palestine between the Arabs and Jews. Thus was born the idea of *partition*. The Jews would get one-fourth of Palestine, including the Galilee, the Jezreel Valley, and the coastal plain. The Arabs would get the rest of Palestine, plus Transjordan. Jerusalem would remain under a permanent British Mandate.

Partition was the first step toward declaring the Jewish state. Yet once again the Jews' hopes for a national homeland were short-lived. Members of Mapai refused to go along with the partition plan to give up most of the Holy Land. The Arab response to partition was to randomly kill any Jew they could find and to call for another strike.[1]

Great Britain responded by ordering the Mufti Haj Amin el-Husseini ousted from Palestine. El-Husseini

Ben-Gurion pledged Jewish support for the defense of Palestine during the Second World War. He is shown here chatting with the British Chief Recruiting Officer for Palestine in 1941.

escaped to Syria, where he directed terrorist activities from across the border. Then an inter-Arab conference threatened that if the British government did not repeal the Balfour Declaration, the Arabs would ally themselves with European nations hostile to Great Britain. In December 1937, the British government officially declared itself no longer bound by the partition plan.[2]

The Haganah and the Irgun began underground rescue operations for Jews trapped in Germany. One of the most courageous was the "Youth Aliyah," started by Recha Freier, a Berlin rabbi's wife, and Henrietta Szold, a Jewish schoolteacher from Baltimore, Maryland. Through their efforts, thousands of Jewish children were smuggled out of Germany. At the same time, Ben-Gurion pleaded with the British to allow just one hundred thousand adult Jews and twenty thousand Jewish children to enter Palestine. Great Britain refused.

In a panic to save their lives, many European Jews tried to find refuge in other countries besides Palestine. But the 1930s had been years of economic depression, and other governments would not take in any more people to feed, house, and employ. A desperate Ben-Gurion ordered the Haganah to sneak German Jews into Palestine regardless of the British restrictions on immigration. His orders were quite clear—"Save them!"[3]

Through the work of the Haganah, almost sixty thousand German Jews were brought into Palestine. The number was not nearly enough. There were three million Jews in Poland, and another estimated three million in the Soviet Union. Ben-Gurion wrote Paula from London that "Hitler's prestige will rise even higher in Germany and the world. America will retreat into its shell and will recoil in disgust from European affairs. The Central European countries will rush to make peace with the Nazis, and a new and terrible threat will confront the Jews of Europe."[4]

Feeling helpless to save more Jews, Ben-Gurion and Chaim Weizmann tried to convince Malcolm MacDonald, who was former Prime Minister Ramsay MacDonald's son, and now the British colonial secretary, to allow more Jews into Palestine. MacDonald said that "Hitler is an intelligent and practical man who wishes to free the Rhine area and to annex Austria and Sudetenland, and nothing more. . . . The arrangement with Hitler ensures peace in the world. . . ."[5]

Weizmann and Ben-Gurion practically went into shock. Then MacDonald added that Great Britain intended to decrease Jewish immigration even further, as the government wanted to maintain a Jewish minority in Palestine for the time being. If a world war erupted, the Moslems might raise their weapons against the British Empire. Ben-Gurion could barely raise himself out of his chair. Enraged that the British were going to sell out the Jews to protect the empire, he ordered the Haganah to form regular military units. Then he sent Haganah agents to European cities to buy more weapons, which they smuggled into Palestine inside iron pipes and barrels of cement.

In 1938, Allied representatives met in Evian, France, to discuss ways to rescue European Jews, and David Ben-Gurion made perhaps the biggest mistake of his life. He did not attend. Although he had appealed to the British to let Europe's Jews into Palestine, he did not want to ask world leaders for a concession that Great Britain had already denied. Such an appeal might antagonize the British, whose friendship Ben-Gurion still believed was vital if Jews were to have their homeland. Moreover, if he spoke out for the plight of Europe's Jews, and Great Britain would not let them come to Palestine, other countries might decide to take them in. And Ben-Gurion wanted those Jews in Palestine, whether now or after the war. He believed partition would eventually be passed, and Jews in Palestine would need to become a majority in order to proclaim a Jewish state.

As a result, David Ben-Gurion missed his best chance to save Europe's Jews. The Allies in Evian were searching for a way to get the Jews out of Hitler's grasp, and Ben-Gurion was the man with the answer. Unable to come up with a workable solution, the Evian Conference was adjourned. It has been argued that Ben-Gurion would have pleaded the Jewish cause to the Allies if he had known what Hitler's "Final Solution" entailed. But, like many Allied leaders, Ben-Gurion had heard only hideously incredible rumors and he had no concrete proof that Hitler planned to murder other Jews in addition to those in Germany.

Even when Hitler gave the world a glimpse of the unbelievable, most people still did not believe such atrocities were happening to Jews. On November 9, 1938, a Polish Jew, enraged by his parents' exile from Germany, shot and killed a German diplomat in Paris. That night, Hitler sent his storm troopers through the streets of Germany to kill Jews. The Nazis broke into almost every Jewish shop and synagogue in Germany. By dawn, hundreds of Jews had been murdered, and forty thousand others had been sent to concentration camps. The streets were covered with broken glass, and the Germans named the night *Kristallnacht*—"the Night of Broken Glass."

In February 1939, Ben-Gurion met with Colonial Secretary Malcolm MacDonald and Arab and Jewish representatives at London's St. James's Palace to discuss the Jewish immigration problem. MacDonald vetoed every suggestion Ben-Gurion made and insisted that the Jews remain a minority within an Arab state. Ben-Gurion was so angry that in a fit of rage he yanked off the velvet gloves he was required to wear in the palace. Then he shouted that ". . . suspension of Jewish immigration will prove impossible without the aid of British bayonets. It will likewise be impossible to convert Palestine into an Arab state against Jewish opposition, without the continuous support of British bayonets!"[6]

Outraged at Ben-Gurion's threats, MacDonald issued the most oppressive "White Paper" against the Jews yet. For the next five years, only fifteen thousand Jews a year could emigrate into Palestine. By 1944, all Jewish immigration into Palestine would cease, unless the Arabs wanted more Jews to enter. The British could deny Jews the right to purchase land in Palestine, and within ten years an independent Arab state would be established. In effect, Great Britain had just canceled the Balfour Declaration.

Meanwhile, Hitler's territorial conquests in Europe were pushing England to the brink of war. In March 1939, Hitler annexed the other half of Czechoslovakia, in violation of the 1938 Munich Conference, which gave Germany half of Czechoslovakia and the Sudetenland. In August 1939, Hitler signed a nonaggression pact with Russia. Even with Hitler's increasing aggression in Europe, by giving him these "little concessions," England's Prime Minister Neville Chamberlain still believed that he was securing "peace in our time."[7]

At the Twenty-first World Zionist Congress in Geneva, Switzerland, in August 1939, a sad Chaim Weizmann said: "There are some things that cannot fail to happen. . . . The remnant shall work on, fight on, live on until the dawn of better days. Towards that dawn I greet you. May we meet again in peace."[8] The hundreds of Jews who attended the conference left with their spirits high, never suspecting that this would be the last World Zionist Congress most of them would live to attend. On September 1, 1939, Hitler invaded Poland, and World War II began. In Poland, the S.S., Hitler's private Nazi storm troopers, had begun to drag Jews out of their homes, businesses, and synagogues and pile them into cattle cars where they were taken to forced labor camps.

SEVEN

★

Enter the Dragon Slayer

When Hitler invaded Poland, many people feared it was too late to save Europe's Jews from annihilation, especially with Great Britain enforcing the White Paper's limitation on Jewish immigration into Palestine. Ben-Gurion, his blue eyes blazing, called an emergency meeting of the Haganah and the Jewish Agency. He said the only way to assure British support for the Jewish state after the war was for the Jewish national army to help the British fight the Nazis. Ben-Gurion declared, "We shall fight the War as if there were no White Paper. But we shall fight the White Paper as if there were no war."[1]

Great Britain, however, would not let the Jews in Palestine form their own army. Therefore, ten thousand Palestinian Jews enlisted in the British army and fought on all fronts. The Haganah alone supplied thirty thousand men, among whom was Ben-Gurion's son, Amos. British soldiers trained Haganah youth to fight the Nazis in Iraq and Syria, and many volunteered to parachute behind German lines to rescue Jews.

Ben-Gurion flew to America to rally U.S. support against the White Paper. He told American statesmen that thousands of Jewish refugees were stranded in small ships anchored in the seas around the world, waiting for a country to take them in. None did. The tragic irony was that many Jews, after finally escaping the Nazis, died on the very boats that were supposedly taking them out of Europe to save them from Hitler's extermination plan.

One of the most tragic cases occurred in 1939 when a group of German Jews on board the SS *St. Louis* sailed to Cuba, where they had been told their visas would be honored. Once there, however, Cuban authorities refused to allow the ship to dock. The captain sailed the ship to the United States, where the refugees met the same response. The *St. Louis* was forced to return to Europe, where three-quarters of the passengers were killed by the Nazis.

Jews on the ship *Struma*, anchored in a port in Istanbul, were refused visas to land in Palestine. The *Struma* was forced out of port in Istanbul into the Black Sea, where an explosion sank the ship, killing all but one of the seven hundred and sixty-four Jews on board.[2]

In 1941, the first fires were ignited in the ovens of Hitler's concentration camps, the Japanese bombed Pearl Harbor, and the United States entered the war. Although the British still opposed a Jewish army, by the end of 1941 the Mandate authorities informally recognized a special Haganah fighting unit, named the *Palmach* (the "Striking Force"), a commando unit of close to three thousand men and women.

In May 1942, Ben-Gurion attended an international Zionist meeting at the Biltmore Hotel in New York City. He proposed and won the passage of a resolution called the "Biltmore Program," which declared that the Balfour Declaration had no further value to the Jews, and included demands that the White Paper be rescinded, a Jewish army be formed, and a Jewish state be established in Palestine.

Then, in June 1942, German General Rommel's Afrika Korps occupied Egypt, putting the Germans at the British

Empire's back door. Great Britain was terrified that the Germans would invade Palestine and proceed to destroy the British Empire. The British wanted an extra defense force to guard Palestinian borders. Therefore, in August 1944, the British War Office established a "Jewish Brigade" as part of the British army, made up of five thousand men, each wearing a Star of David arm patch as his insignia. Although the Jewish Brigade fought for only a few months at the end of the Allied campaign in Italy, it was able to send many Holocaust survivors to Palestine as illegal immigrants, which helped to establish the needed Jewish majority in Palestine.

Meanwhile, the two Revisionist groups in Palestine, the Irgun, now led by Menachem Begin after Jabotinsky's death in 1940, and the Stern group, named after its leader, Avraham Stern, launched a series of anti-British terrorist actions. The Irgun blew up British intelligence headquarters throughout Palestine, attacked police stations, and assassinated British officers.

In November 1944, Winston Churchill asked Chaim Weizmann to meet in Cairo with Lord Moyne, the resident British minister in the Middle East. Although Moyne was known for his anti-Zionist sentiments, he had finally agreed to the idea of partition. However, before the meeting took place, the Stern group, unaware of Lord Moyne's change in attitude, murdered him. Ben-Gurion was mortified. He warned the militant groups to halt all terrorism or he would wipe them out.

The Stern group capitulated, but Menachem Begin refused to put the Irgun under the authority of Haganah commanders unless they declared war on Great Britain. Ben-Gurion, who never took threats lightly, passed a law making terrorist activities illegal. He had scored only a temporary victory, however, as the law left unresolved the opposing beliefs and tensions between the Haganah and the Irgun. Later, this friction would explode in harmful ways during the struggle for Jewish statehood.

Grief followed Ben-Gurion's satisfaction with his

counterterrorist resolution. While in London, he received a cable from Paula telling him his father had died. Avigdor Green was eighty-seven. David wrote Paula: "In my loneliness, far from home, comes this saddening news. From my father I inherited my love of the Jewish people, of the Land of Israel and of the Hebrew language. . . ."[3]

More sad news followed when Berl Katzenelson died unexpectedly. Ben-Gurion considered him the only true friend he had, and later wrote in his diary that, "The burden of this grief will bear me down until my dying day. . . ."[4] With Katzenelson's death, Ben-Gurion no longer had anyone to help keep his impulsive acts in check, and he became the sole leader of his party.

By April 1945 the German offensive against Russia had collapsed, and the Allies closed in on Germany. Inside his underground bunker in Berlin, Adolf Hitler put a gun to his head and shot himself. On May 8, Germany surrendered and World War II ended.

Europe was a Jewish graveyard. Ben-Gurion mourned the dead and berated himself for not believing in the existence of the death camps sooner. Out of seven and a half million Jews living in Europe before the war, Hitler's Nazis had murdered six million. The survivors, near death themselves, were taken to camps for Displaced Persons, while the Red Cross and other volunteers tried to find their relatives, or relocate them somewhere else. These camps were often former concentration camps, merely renamed, but with the same high watchtowers and barbed wire circling the grounds.

Ben-Gurion visited several DP camps and was horrified to see the survivors with their bones protruding from their flesh like living skeletons. When he returned to Jerusalem, he told others what he had seen:

I was in Dachau and Bergen-Belsen. I saw . . . the gallows . . . where Jews were hanged . . . racks whereon Jewish men and women were stretched out naked

to be shot at by warders . . . the gas chambers . . .
made as if there were showers in them. . . . From the
tragic few miraculously saved, I bring two prayers.
One, for the unity of Israel. The second, for a Jewish
State, a call that goes out from the dead millions to
surviving Jewry and the conscience of the world.[5]

The world listened. International statesmen and world leaders, to ease their guilty consciences for having ignored the plight of Europe's Jews, now wanted to help the Zionists. Yet Great Britain still refused to let Jewish refugees into Palestine. Moreover, to make sure no Jews were smuggled in, the British Fleet blockaded the Middle East coast, intercepted illegal boatfuls of refugees, and sent them to detention camps in Cyprus.

In response, Ben-Gurion ordered the Haganah, Irgun, and Stern groups to smuggle refugees past the blockade. The groups complied, and in the process joined forces to form the Hebrew Resistance movement. Ben-Gurion believed the British Mandate would shortly end, and as soon as British troops left Palestine, the Arabs would launch their threatened attack on the Jews, who would have to defend themselves without British protection. When this Holy War was declared, he wanted the Jews prepared. At the age of sixty, David Ben-Gurion was again changing his career, this time from politician to military strategist.

The Jews desperately needed money to buy modern weapons if they were going to defend themselves against the Arabs. Ben-Gurion decided to ask wealthy American Jews for financial support. In the summer of 1945, he flew to New York where he asked the assistance of Rudolf Sonneborn, a wealthy Zionist. Through Sonneborn's efforts, Jewish statesmen and businessmen all over the United States agreed to help.

In order to keep their contributions secret, the donors adopted the name "The Sonneborn Institute." They worked with Haganah agents in the United States to set up dummy corporations that would buy government surplus weapons from any source they could find, including the Mafia. American gambling casinos even donated a percentage of their profits to the Jewish cause. In Palestine, the institute built an underground ammunition plant. Soon branches of the Sonneborn Institute appeared in several European cities. During the next few years, the institute sent millions of dollars to Palestine.

In October 1945, the Hebrew Resistance movement raided the Atlith detention camp, setting free two hundred illegal immigrants. In November, the movement sabotaged the railroad in Palestine and blew up British coastguard vessels. The British retaliated by putting Palestine under martial law and sending in two thousand more troops to keep order. The British soldiers hanged all the Jewish insurgents they caught.

June 29, 1946, would always be remembered by the Jews as "Black Saturday." British troops entered Jewish villages in tanks and armored cars. Jews frantically tried to phone for help, but their lines were dead. The British troops broke into Jewish homes and ripped up floors and walls searching for hidden weapons. Then the soldiers dragged Jews outside, locked them in cages, and sent them to detention camps. Once there, many Jews were tortured and even killed.

Ben-Gurion was appalled at the needless deaths. In a desperate move, he approved a plan for the Hebrew Resistance movement to blow up the King David Hotel in Jerusalem, which was the headquarters of the British provisional government. Then, the day before the scheduled explosion, Ben-Gurion realized the price in British retaliation would be too high, and he rescinded his order.

Menachem Begin and his Irgun ignored Ben-Gurion's order and planted the bomb inside a large milk can in the hotel. The explosion shook all of Jerusalem. As flames shot out of the King David's roof, British officials and hotel guests scrambled in all directions trying to escape. When the fire was extinguished, almost a hundred people had died.

Ben-Gurion was livid. The terrorist act signaled the end

of the Hebrew Resistance movement. Many Zionists returned to moderate Chaim Weizmann for leadership, and the *Yishuv* split in their loyalty between Weizmann and Ben-Gurion. To maintain his position as leader of all Zionism, Ben-Gurion tried to appease both the moderates and liberals in the World Zionist Organization. He decided the best way to compete with Weizmann was to get rid of the man without humiliating him.

In December 1946, in Basel, Switzerland, the first postwar World Zionist Congress was held. Ben-Gurion suggested that Chaim Weizmann step down as president and become "honorary" president of the World Zionist Organization. The delegates, believing they needed Ben-Gurion to push for a Jewish state and to lead them against Arab attacks, voted for Weizmann to step down. He was forced to accept since Ben-Gurion threatened to resign if he refused.

Now Ben-Gurion felt he was in a stronger position to bargain with British Foreign Secretary Ernest Bevin for a Jewish state in Palestine. Ben-Gurion warned Bevin that if war broke out between Arabs and Jews, Great Britain would be caught in the middle. Flustered, Bevin reluctantly agreed with other British Parliament members that the Balfour Declaration was useless. He blurted out that the United Nations could decide what to do with Palestine.

In February 1947, the UN debated the Palestine issue. While Ben-Gurion waited for the decision, he occupied himself with defense preparations against an anticipated all-out Arab attack on the Jews. The best guerrilla unit was the Palmach, but it belonged to his opposition party, Mapam, formed by the leftists who resigned from Mapai in 1944. The Haganah, on the other hand, was accustomed to the short skirmishes of guerrilla warfare, but not to fighting an attack by a regular army. Ben-Gurion asked Chaim Laskov, a Jewish Brigade veteran, to train the Haganah in modern fighting methods.

In June 1947, the UN General Assembly created a United Nations Special Committee on Palestine (UN-

SCOP) to investigate Arab and Jewish claims to the Holy Land. Ben-Gurion told the committee that there was only one way to guarantee another Holocaust would not happen to the Jews. That was to let them create a Jewish homeland and a state. The committee thought that Ben-Gurion's logic made sense, and then the British unknowingly pushed UNSCOP the rest of the way into favoring a Jewish state by broadcasting the pitiful condition of Holocaust survivors.

Under orders from Foreign Secretary Bevin, British troops refused to allow the *Exodus*, a ship from France carrying 4,554 Jewish refugees, to land in Haifa. The captain tried to outrun British patrol boats and dock anyway, but one of the boats rammed the ship and ferried it to Haifa. When the British soldiers attempted to board, the refugees fought them off, and the British opened fire. Three Jews were killed and many others were wounded. Bevin ordered the *Exodus* to return to France, but when the ship arrived, the refugees refused to disembark. The captain was forced to dock in Hamburg, Germany. There the Jews were returned to the same DP camps they had fled only a few weeks before.

The *Exodus* story made world headlines. People everywhere, including UNSCOP, whose members decided that Palestine should be partitioned into two states, felt that the British action was intolerable. The Arabs would receive the west bank of the Jordan, the western Galilee, the Gaza Strip, and an Egyptian-Sinai border zone; the Jews would receive the Negev desert, the eastern Galilee, and the coastline north of Haifa to the Gaza Strip. Jerusalem would remain an international zone under a UN trusteeship, with Jews and Arabs participating in its local government. Now two-thirds of the UN General Assembly had to vote in favor of the measure before partition could be implemented.

Ben-Gurion felt optimistic that partition would pass, but he was careful not to let his belief that the Jewish state was about to become a reality blind him from defense preparations against the eventual Arab attack. He called on Golda Myerson, the same young woman who many years

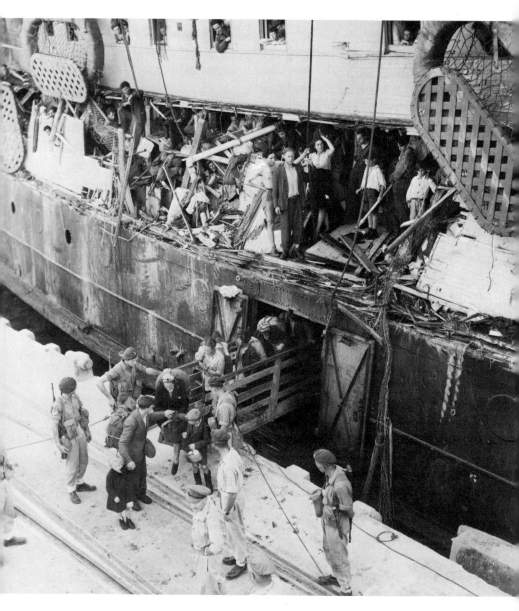

Jewish refugees leaving the Exodus at Haifa docks in Palestine in 1947. The illegal immigration ship from Europe was intercepted and rammed in the hull by British naval forces after a fierce battle.

ago had called his speech in Milwaukee, Wisconsin, boring. Golda Myerson was now an important figure in the women's Zionist movement in Palestine. Ben-Gurion asked her to persuade King Abdullah of Transjordan not to take any action against the Jews. Golda managed to see Abdullah, and reported that he would keep the Arab armies from attacking the Jews if the Jews would let Abdullah take over the Arab portion of the partitioned state.

On November 29, 1947, the United Nations General Assembly cast its votes for partition. Jews in Palestine listened to loudspeakers set up in the streets. When the last vote was called, the count was thirty-three nations in favor of partition, thirteen against. The Jews burst into cheers, singing and dancing in the streets of Palestine.

At his home in Jerusalem, David Ben-Gurion shuffled to his desk and started to write. When he ran out of paper, he wrote on brown toilet tissue that, "The Jewish people . . . will not fall short at this great hour of the opportunity and the historic responsibility that have been given to it. The restored Judea will take an honorable place in the Holy Land, the Near East and the world at large."[6]

The day after the UN vote, the Arabs rejected partition; Great Britain refused to assist the UN in carrying out the plan; and many Zionists voiced their dissatisfaction with the small area given to the Jews. Then the Arabs attacked, and Ben-Gurion knew that once again the time had not yet arrived when Jews could "beat their swords into plow-shares."

Golda Myerson flew to the United States to ask American Jews for money to help the Israelis buy more weapons and supplies. In the meantime, Arabs broke into Jewish shops and set them on fire. Then they took over the Old City of Jerusalem, blowing up a block of houses, and bombed the *Palestine Post*, one of the leading English-language newspapers in Jerusalem. The Old City fell deadly silent as Jews stayed indoors, afraid if they went outside they would be shot by Arab snipers.

Next the Arabs took over the road to Jerusalem, cutting

off the city's communications and supplies, and leaving one hundred thousand Jews trapped without food or water. By January 1948, the Arab holy war was growing more violent each day. The United Nations, without a police force to back up its decisions, hesitated to enforce the partition plan.

Ben-Gurion sank into depression, feeling alone against the increasing opposition to Jewish statehood. Yet in the midst of his depression, he received word that a Czechoslovakian arms firm was willing to supply everything on his defense supply list. More good news followed when Golda Myerson returned from New York with fifty million dollars, much more than they had expected. In addition, the Palmach started sneaking into Arab territories at night, blowing up their headquarters and stealing their weapons. And under Chaim Laskov's direction, the Haganah became a highly skilled attack force. Morale soared as the Haganah drove Arab forces from Haifa, Tiberias, and Safad, and many Moslem villagers fled to Arab border towns.

The British Mandate was scheduled to end on May 15, 1948. Ben-Gurion realized that if he did not declare the Jewish area of Palestine a state now, he might never again have the chance. He called a meeting of Zionists to appoint a provisional government of two bodies, the National Council and the National Administration. When the Mandate ended, these bodies would serve as a temporary Jewish Parliament until official elections were held. Ben-Gurion was made both temporary prime minister and defense minister of the provisional government.

On April 1, Ben-Gurion ordered the Jewish army to take over all areas of Palestine granted them by partition. Then he ordered Haganah chiefs to storm the village of Kastel above the road to Jerusalem. With Kastel occupied, the road to Jerusalem could be reopened and fresh supplies brought in. At dawn on April 3, fifteen hundred Haganah fighters and Palmach commandos seized Kastel.

When the leaders of the Stern and Irgun groups heard about the Haganah's victory at Kastel, they were jealous of their rival army's success, and decided to wipe out an Arab target of their own. Their leaders warned the villagers in Deir Yassin, a village outside Jerusalem, to leave. Then the terrorist groups stormed the village. When the Arabs started shooting back, the Jews dynamited the houses and gunned down Arab men, women, and children at random. More than two hundred Arabs were killed.

Ben-Gurion was furious with the terrorist groups for attacking the Arab village without provocation. King Abdullah blamed the Jews for the slaughter and backed out of his agreement. As a result, hundreds of thousands more Arabs fled Palestine. The Arab population in Palestine thus decreased enough to make the Jews a majority in the Holy Land, which was the British condition for the Jews to claim Palestine a Jewish state.

The remaining Arabs sought revenge for Deir Yassin. They bombed buses on their way up Mount Scopus to the Hebrew University and Hadassah Hospital above Jerusalem. Ben-Gurion burst into tears when he heard the fiancé of his daughter Renana was on one of the buses. The United Nations called for a truce in which Jews and Arabs would rule their own communities without declaring a state. Ben-Gurion rejected the truce as it went against the UN partition plan, which specified a Jewish state.

On May 12, three days before British troops were scheduled to leave Palestine, Ben-Gurion, his face haggard and dark circles outlining his eyes, called a meeting of the provisional government. He told members that when the Arabs attacked, at least sixty thousand Jews would be killed. Then he asked them to vote on the UN truce plan. If the provisional government voted against the truce, Ben-Gurion would declare a Jewish state.

The air in the room seemed to crackle with electricity as the men cast their votes. Ben-Gurion's heart pounded as he tallied them up. Then he smiled. The results were six to four against the truce. Ben-Gurion's dream was about to come true.

EIGHT

✦

Another David,
Another Goliath

We, members of the People's Council, representatives of the Jewish community of Eretz-Israel *and of the Zionist movement . . . by virtue of our natural and historic right, and on the strength of the Resolution of the United Nations General Assembly, hereby declare the establishment of a Jewish State in* Eretz-Israel, *to be known as the State of Israel.*[1]

With these words, David Ben-Gurion officially proclaimed the Jewish state of Israel. The date was May 14, 1948. Forty-two years had passed since David Green had arrived in Palestine on an overcrowded freighter. Declaring the creation of the Jewish state was a bold and risky step in light of the impending Arab attack. As Ben-Gurion later said, "I don't know of anyone in the Provisional Government who wasn't tortured by second thoughts."[2]

Although the meeting was supposed to be secret, reporters discovered the story and arrived at the Tel Aviv Museum of Art with their cameras and microphones ready.

*Israeli state officials listen to David Ben-Gurion's
proclamation to the world declaring the birth of
the state of Israel. The portrait behind Ben-Gurion
is that of Zionism's founder, Theodor Herzl.
At last, on May 14, 1948, a destiny was fulfilled.*

At the museum's entrance, the newly designed Israeli flag, with its Star of David symbolizing King David's shield in the middle of two blue and white stripes, seemed to wave in triumph. Behind the dais in the auditorium hung a portrait of Theodor Herzl, who had predicted this day fifty-one years earlier. At exactly four o'clock in the afternoon, everyone stood and sang *Hatikvah* ("The Hope"), which had been chosen as Israel's national anthem.

Then David Ben-Gurion walked to the microphone, and the voices hushed. In those few seconds, the auditorium seemed to fill with the presence of others, as if the spirits of all Jews, from ancient times to the recent victims of the Holocaust, had penetrated the walls to take their rightful places among the living. For the spirits, too, had fought for this day. David Ben-Gurion's blue eyes glistened with tears as he finished reading the proclamation. Then shouts of "Mazel-Tov" sent the auditorium into a frenzy of hands clapping, feet stomping, and bodies embracing. After two thousand years of struggle, the Jews had finally reclaimed their Holy Land.

At the stroke of midnight, the last British ship, the *Euryalus*, left Haifa, ending thirty years of British rule over Palestine. At 12:01 A.M., Egyptian planes bombed Tel Aviv. At 12:10 A.M., U.S. President Harry Truman recognized Israel as a state. Recognition by Guatemala and the Soviet Union followed within days.

By dawn, the Arabs were invading Israel from every border. The Old City of Jerusalem was hit by ten thousand Arab shells, obliterating the city's Jewish Quarter, along with many of the oldest Arab and Jewish artifacts in the world. While the secretary general of the Arab League announced the Arabs would fight a "Lightning War," in which they would push the Jews into the Mediterranean, Ben-Gurion anxiously awaited the arrival of the arms shipment from Czechoslovakia. He felt as if he were the biblical David fighting the giant Goliath, as he ordered the Israelis not to give up one kibbutz or one square inch of land to the Arabs.

That same afternoon, every able-bodied Jew in Palestine enlisted in the army. Without modern arms, they improvised weapons such as Molotov cocktails and farm tools. The Israeli air force, having only single-engine planes, mounted the planes with machine guns. "Bombing the enemy" was lobbing a grenade out of the cockpit. Outnumbered by the enemy, but filled with national spirit, the Jews drove the Arabs out of Beersheba.

The tiny new nation was fast turning the Arab "Lightning War" into a slow-burning candle. To win the war, Ben-Gurion believed Israel needed to unify its armies. He passed a resolution through the provisional government abolishing the old high command of the Haganah and replacing it with a hierarchy of command posts, each with its own commander. Ben-Gurion named himself commander in chief. He appointed Lieutenant Colonel Moshe Dayan military commander of Jerusalem.

Next Ben-Gurion dissolved the Palmach into the new army. In spite of the Stern group's and the Irgun's refusal to join ranks, the merger of the other military groups was sufficient to establish a unified army. Thus the Israel Defense Forces (IDF) came into being. With the arrival of almost five thousand Jewish immigrants by the second week of Israel's statehood, the force swelled to sixty thousand men. Today the IDF is a highly trained army, navy, and air force, and is admired as one of the most skilled combat forces in the world.

On May 23, the arms shipment from Czechoslovakia arrived, and shortly thereafter King Abdullah's troops occupied the road to Jerusalem. Ben-Gurion pored over old maps of the area searching for an alternate route into the city. Then he ordered what has been called the only major mistake in the War of Independence. In spite of his military advisers' warnings that his plan was too risky, Ben-Gurion ordered the army to capture Latrun, a village above the Jerusalem-Tel Aviv Road. After three unsuccessful attempts, and the loss of many Jewish lives, Ben-Gurion withdrew his order and sought an alternate route. Finally he spotted a road on the map heading down a rocky hillside.

For the next five nights, Jewish soldiers and civilians carved a road out of the rocks. They called the route their "Burma Road," after the road built by the Allies during World War II. On June 11 the road was finished. Then Jewish soldiers attacked the Arab forces in Jerusalem and recaptured the city.

Nevertheless, Ben-Gurion felt guilty that he alone had pushed Israelis into the "Battle of Jerusalem," as the siege came to be called, and for asking Israel's young people to fight a war with incredible odds against victory. He dreaded writing letters informing parents of a son's or daughter's death. To one bereaved father, he wrote, "Every Jew in the world is happy about the victories . . . there has been no joy in my house, for I see before me always these precious sons."[3]

The Arab spirit buckled from their defeat in Jerusalem. That same day both sides accepted a four-week truce called by the United Nations, during which time no new military supplies could be brought into Palestine, and neither side could rearm itself. The United Nations sent Count Bernadotte, head of the Swedish Red Cross, to act as a mediator in discussing a possible peace settlement, but neither country accepted his proposals.

One of the most difficult decisions Ben-Gurion made during the war concerned a shipload of arms ordered by the Irgun from France. The Irgun threatened to unload the shipment—transported by the SS *Altalena*—due to dock in Tel Aviv. Ben-Gurion warned the Irgun's leader, Menachem Begin, that such action would break the truce agreement and constitute treason to the Israeli government, which had agreed to abide by the truce. Moreover, the new state needed to show the world it was mature enough to abide by international law.

Begin ignored Ben-Gurion's warning, and an Irgun team started unloading the weapons. Ben-Gurion realized he had to take violent action if he wanted Israel to become a model nation for the world. In a cracking voice, he ordered the Israeli army to blow up the *Altalena*. Fifteen men were killed in the blazing inferno. The incident almost caused a civil war, as Jews fought Jews on Tel Aviv's beaches.

Finally the Irgunists surrendered, and Israel's integrity was clearly shown to the United Nations. In a report to the Provisional State Council, Ben-Gurion said, "To burn the ship was the most loyal service we could render the Yishuv."[4]

The Arabs, on the other hand, did violate the truce by allowing foreign soldiers to enlist in their armies and by attacking Jewish settlements before the cease-fire ended. Ben-Gurion called for an all-out offensive against the Arabs, and ten days later the Arabs called for another cease-fire. More violence followed, however, when UN mediator Count Bernadotte proposed to give the Moslems the Negev Desert and Jerusalem, which the Jews had fought hard to capture from the Arabs. Several members of the Stern group became so angry that they assassinated him.

Ben-Gurion fumed with anger and indignation that the incident would cause the world to view the Israelis as cold-blooded murderers. He had an act passed that outlawed all terrorist groups, which caused the final breakup of the Irgun group, but not the Sternists. As indignation over Count Bernadotte's murder quieted, the Sternists resumed their terrorist activities.

That fall, the Egyptians broke the truce by refusing to allow Israeli convoys to carry food to the besieged Jewish settlements. On October 14, Ben-Gurion ordered the Israeli army to turn its gunfire on Egypt. By December 31, the Israelis had driven the Egyptians out of the Negev back to the Gaza Strip, and had forced the Arab armies out of Jerusalem.

By January 1949, the Egyptians had asked for an

armistice, and Israel had won both the war and its independence. Some four thousand Jewish soldiers and two thousand Jewish civilians had died in the war. On February 24, a truce accord was signed between Israel and Egypt. By July 20, Lebanon, Jordan, and Syria had reached armistice agreements with Israel.

According to the settlement, Jerusalem would be divided into two sections, an Old City within the Western Wall, and a New City outside the Wall. King Abdullah would get the Old City, in addition to the West Bank of the Jordan River. Israel would get the New City, in addition to all the territories the Israelis captured during the war. Egypt would retain the Gaza Strip. The peace terms left no unoccupied Palestinian territory for the creation of any new Arab state. This fact angered the 751,000 Palestinian Arab refugees who had fled Israel during the war and who now lived in squalid refugee camps inside Arab territory, since the United Nations had previously offered them territory in Palestine after the war.

When the Israelis and Arabs met at Lausanne, Switzerland, to turn the peace agreements into official peace treaties, an argument erupted over what to do about the Arab refugees. Israel offered to take in one hundred thousand, but the Arabs insisted Israel take all of the refugees. The Jews refused, and no peace treaty was signed. Then the Arabs expressed their continued hatred of the Jews by voting against Israel's membership in the United Nations. Nevertheless, on May 11, 1949, the UN General Assembly passed a resolution accepting Israel into the United Nations as its fifty-ninth member.

Ben-Gurion now focused his attention on changing the provisional government into a permanent one. Today Israel is still the democratic republic that Ben-Gurion and his colleagues established. The republic consists of a one-chamber parliament, called the *Knesset*, whose one hundred and twenty members are elected by proportional representation. Although there is a president of Israel, he or she has little executive power. The actual running of the government is handled by the political party having a majority of members in the Knesset. The head of this party becomes Israel's prime minister.

Israel's electoral system of proportional representation permits many different political parties to hold seats in the Knesset at one time. Israel's first parliamentary election was held on January 25, 1949. Out of twenty-one parties running candidates for election, representatives from eight different parties were elected to the Knesset. Ben-Gurion's Mapai party won the majority of representatives, and thus David Ben-Gurion became Israel's first prime minister. However, with representatives from so many different political parties sitting in the Knesset, Ben-Gurion faced major hurdles getting his resolutions passed. He tried to convince the smaller parties to join Mapai, but they refused.

Chaim Weizmann was elected the new nation's first president. When he took the oath of office at the first Knesset meeting ever held, he said, "I know that all we do or fail to do in this country will cast light or shadow on our whole people."[5]

For years afterward, Israelis would speak of the courage shown by the tiny Jewish army, which, armed with small arms and farm tools, held on to every kibbutz and every square inch of their land. And people everywhere would hail David Ben-Gurion as the modern David who killed a modern Goliath seven times his size.

NINE

★

Survival of a Nation

For Prime Minister David Ben-Gurion, the fulfillment of his dream signaled the beginning of headaches. Even before the War of Independence ended, he had already started work on his goal of getting more Jews to emigrate to Israel, which he called the "Gathering in of the Exiles." In spite of Mapai's and his cabinet's fears that taking in hundreds of thousands of people every year would mean the collapse of the new state, Ben-Gurion managed to get passed a resolution called the "Law of Return," which allowed unrestricted immigration into Israel. By 1949, Jewish immigrants were arriving in Israel a the rate of one thousand per week, and the population of the new nation soared to one million.

The government's efforts to feed, house, and employ the new arrivals caused an economic depression. Some newcomers lived in the houses vacated by the Arabs, but most had to live in tin huts, with no electricity or plumbing, until the government could find them adequate housing. The immigrants were shocked to discover that the *Eretz Israel* they had dreamed about was mostly wilderness. Many immigrants packed their belongings and left.

Ben-Gurion was saddened to see the immigrants leave, as he knew their poverty was only temporary. He was also disappointed that many of the remaining Jews chose to settle in the big cities, rather than in the undeveloped areas, especially the Negev Desert.

The Negev stretches from the Red Sea in the south, to the Mediterranean Sea in the north, to the Dead Sea in the east, and to the Sinai Peninsula in the west. Ben-Gurion believed that Israel's economic survival depended upon cultivating every inch of land. In 1949, Israel had not discovered enough natural resources to form an export industry, which would help save the depressed economy. Ben-Gurion insisted that buried beneath the sands of the Negev lay hidden treasures which, if unearthed, would provide these resources. On Ben-Gurion's orders, Israeli geologists had already found rich mineral deposits in the desert area of King Solomon's copper mines and were now exploring the Dead Sea, the richest source of mineral salts in the world.

Most members of the Knesset disagreed with Ben-Gurion, and considered the Negev wasteland. Ben-Gurion argued that one pipeline could be laid to irrigate the land and provide drinking water, and another would extend from the Gulf of Eilat into the oil-producing regions of the Middle East. In addition, Jewish settlements in the Negev were vital to protect the state's borders against fedayeen (Arab commandos) suicide raids. Ben-Gurion predicted there would come a time when the conflict between Arabs and Jews would force Israel to need a seaport on the Red Sea. The Gulf of Eilat in the southern desert region would provide this seaport. He firmly believed that the Negev could become the industrial and agricultural heart of Israel. Privately, however, he wondered how he would ever convince enough Jews to move there.

Another problem Ben-Gurion faced was the United Nations' plan to internationalize Jerusalem. In Ben-Gurion's opinion, this plan was nullified when the Arabs broke the cease-fire agreement and attacked Israel. To prove he meant business, Ben-Gurion moved the Knesset's headquarters from Tel Aviv to the New City of Jerusalem. He now had two offices, one in Tel Aviv, where he wore the hat of defense minister, and the other in Jerusalem, where he served as prime minister.

At sixty-three years old, Ben-Gurion still worked from early morning until late at night. Except for the occasional Sabbaths he and Paula spent with their children and grandchildren, the Ben-Gurions had no social life. The prime minister's only form of relaxation was reading or visiting with Rachel and her family.

Paula resented these visits, as she had long ago guessed David's feelings about Rachel. Paula believed all that kept David from leaving her and marrying Rachel was the fact that Rachel was already married. Yet Paula never confronted David about Rachel, for, on the other hand, she enjoyed all the attention given her as the prime minister's wife. Paula especially liked attending state functions where she met presidents, kings, and queens.

She was an outspoken woman and said anything she felt like to whomever she wanted, much to the embarrassment of foreign diplomats and members of the Knesset. Once, at a state dinner, she told Dag Hammarskjöld, the United Nations secretary-general, he should get married. When Hammarskjöld asked why, Paula answered, "Married people have trouble . . . with the children and . . . making a living. You would have so much trouble of your own, you wouldn't have time to give us any!"[1] When someone asked her how her husband should be addressed, Paula answered, "Call him Ben-Gurion. Anyone can be a Prime Minister, but not everyone can be a Ben-Gurion."[2]

Although Ben-Gurion worked practically twenty-four hours a day, he spent part of each day visiting the immigrant settlements to personally welcome the new Jews to Israel. The immigrants immediately liked the short, frizzy-haired gentleman with the kind smile, who shook each of their hands. Most Israelis called him "B.G.," and thought of him as their Messiah. Not one blamed Ben-Gurion for Israel's problems. Instead, they accused other members of Parliament.

The immigrant Jews blamed two groups in particular, who were perhaps the only Israelis who did not view Ben-Gurion as their Messiah. These groups were members of Mapai's two rival political parties, the left-wing Mapam, which supported Russian dictator Joseph Stalin in all his Communist policies except anti-Zionism, and Menachem Begin's Herut party, formed when Begin split with the Irgun.

For the time being, however, Ben-Gurion had to put aside his problems with the rival political parties. Israel's depressed economy had to be dealt with first; it needed one billion dollars to save itself from bankruptcy. Once again, Ben-Gurion asked American Jews for assistance. Jacob Blaustein, president of the American Jewish Committee, agreed to help.

In May 1951, David and Paula flew to New York to initiate the first Israeli Bond Drive. Americans would buy Israeli bonds, which would be paid back to them with interest after a certain time period. In only two weeks, American Jews bought fifty-five million dollars worth of Israeli bonds, and Ben-Gurion returned to Israel triumphant.

Ben-Gurion's elation over the successful bond drive was dampened when he learned that in his absence, Arab terrorists had killed King Abdullah of Jordan and the prime minister of Lebanon for talking to Ben-Gurion. As a result, other Arab leaders hesitated to speak to Ben-Gurion, fearing they too would be murdered. Thus peace negotiations between Israel, Jordan, and Lebanon ended.

The failed peace efforts were followed by a political

In 1951, Ben-Gurion as Prime Minister of the first
Israeli government, toured the United States to
promote the first Israeli Bond Drive. In addition to
meeting with many American dignitaries and businessmen,
Ben-Gurion also visited many famous Jewish entertainers
and intellectuals living in the United States. Here he is
shown with celebrated physicist Albert Einstein (left).

victory for Ben-Gurion when war broke out between North and South Korea. At U.S. President Truman's request, Ben-Gurion and his Mapai party agreed to support United Nations Forces in aiding South Korea against the Communist North Koreans, who were backed by the Soviet Union. Mapam, on the other hand, supported Stalin and North Korea. Then, in 1952, the Israeli secret service reported that Mapam members had stolen secret Mapai military documents, and that Communists, without Mapam's knowledge, had infiltrated the party.

Mapam members were disgraced when Ben-Gurion confronted them with these facts. Yet they received a worse blow when Stalin realized that Israel would never join forces with Russia. For them, Communist Czechoslovakia felt free to try eleven Jews for allegedly plotting to overthrow the Czech government. One of the Jews was a Mapam member. At a Knesset meeting, Ben-Gurion lashed out at Mapam for failing to recognize Stalin's anti-Semitism, and the Mapam party fell apart under the pressure. Ben-Gurion was thus left with only one rival party in the Knesset, Menachem Begin's Herut party.

That same year, a military coup ousted Egypt's King Farouk. He was replaced by Gamal Abdel Nasser, a young army colonel. Nasser spoke out against the United Nations for allowing the Jews to establish the state of Israel. He wrote a book titled *The Philosophy of the Revolution*, in which he vowed to create a Nasser-ruled Arab country, stretching from Syria to the African continent. He started to work on his new country by increasing fedayeen attacks on Israeli villages. Hundreds of Israelis were killed.

In retaliation, Ben-Gurion ordered an army unit led by Ariel Sharon, a highly skilled fighter, to invade the Jordanian village of Kibya. The Jewish soldiers arrived to find the village seemingly deserted. They dynamited all the houses, destroying Kibya, but also seventy settlers who were hiding in one of the houses. The world condemned Israel's action. To save the name of the army, Ben-Gurion said that Israelis living on the Jordanian border were angry over fedayeen raids into their villages, and had fought back on their own.

Adding trouble on top of trouble, the Israeli bond sales were not bringing in enough money to save the economy. Aware that he would face bitter opposition, Ben-Gurion nevertheless submitted a claim to West Germany for one and a half billion dollars in reparations. These reparations had previously been negotiated by American, British, and Israeli governments on behalf of the Holocaust survivors. Many Jews criticized Israel for negotiating with the Germans so soon after the war. Ben-Gurion, however, believed he was only asking for compensation for Jewish property that was confiscated by the Nazis.

He ordered Jewish Agency Chairman Nahum Goldmann, to "see West German Chancellor Konrad Adenauer and ask for a billion dollars."[3] Goldmann obeyed, and was stunned when Adenauer offered to give Israel one billion dollars. Menachem Begin and his Herut party accused Ben-Gurion of accepting "blood money" and incited a crowd of Jews to storm the Knesset. In defiance of Herut's violence, the Knesset passed the reparations agreement.

In November 1952, Israeli President Chaim Weizmann died, and Ben-Gurion's cherished friend, Yitzhak Ben-Zvi, was elected Israel's second president.

Ben-Gurion, at the age of sixty-seven, had now spent fifty years in Palestine. He felt he needed time off to rest. In November 1953, at the peak of his career, David Ben-Gurion shocked Israelis by announcing his retirement as prime minister. He would, however, keep his seat in the Knesset while he took a two-year leave of absence. When he was begged to change his mind, he answered that, "No man is indispensable. The more a statesman is in power, the greater the danger of his becoming too self-assured so that he deals lightly with heavy and complicated problems."[4]

Privately Ben-Gurion hoped his moving to the desert would set an example to other Israelis to follow him. In the meantime, Moshe Sharett, Israeli foreign minister, would serve as interim prime minister until new elections were held in August. Ben-Gurion promised he would not leave until he made sure Israel would be in good hands during his absence.

While Ben-Gurion prepared to retire, an incident occurred one afternoon that changed his life. While returning from business in the town of Eilat, his driver had to go through a desert pass. Suddenly Ben-Gurion shouted for him to pull off the road. The startled driver stopped the car, hoping the prime minister would not linger, as the pass was inhabited by Bedouins who attacked Jews.

Ben-Gurion was not afraid. He had seen some Byzantine ruins at the side of the road and wanted to take a closer look. He marveled that less than two thousand years ago the Nabatean culture had flourished on this very spot. They had irrigated the land by building stone walls at the end of the sloping fields to hold the little rain water that fell. As he studied the ruins, some young men and women approached him. Dressed in khaki shorts and shirts, they walked with a small herd of sheep, using rifles as staffs.

One of the men said they were veterans from Israel's War of Independence, and had come to build a kibbutz, the term for an Israeli collective farm, in the desert. A yearning stirred inside Ben-Gurion, but he could not give it a name. The men and women showed him their primitive settlement of scattered huts and tin sheds, which held some lambs. They had named the kibbutz Sdeh Boker, meaning "Shepherd's Field."

Unknowingly, Ben-Gurion had just taken his first glimpse of the kibbutz where he would spend the last years of his life. He felt deep pride in these young people, who were making a "flower blossom in the desert." All at once Ben-Gurion knew what the yearning was inside him. Sdeh Boker reminded him of the farm in the Sejera region of the Galilee that he had loved so much. Now he also knew where he wanted to live during his two-year absence from the Knesset.

Paula thought he was crazy when he told her he wanted to give up their modern life-style and go live in the desert. Her reaction was to become obsessed with supplying David's every need. Each night, she laid out his clothes for the next day. She cooked his meals in hotel kitchens, and told the airlines he flew on what to serve him on flights. Paula said she *had* to go with David to Sdeh Boker. Who else would keep him from catching cold, make sure he ate well-balanced meals, or protect him from snakebites?

When David told the people at Sdeh Boker about his plans, they were astonished that the prime minister of Israel would want to live in such poverty. Nonsense, he told them. "After all, there is room for only one prime minister, but for those who make the desert bloom, there is room for hundreds, thousands, and even millions."[5] Nevertheless, the kibbutzniks insisted on building him a decent house. They assembled a prefabricated cottage, with a water tank outside. Without a water pipeline, the kibbutzniks trucked in water from Bersheeba, thirty miles away.

On December 13, 1953, David and Paula arrived at Sdeh Boker, and were given a warm welcome. Then the manager of the kibbutz showed Ben-Gurion a daily worksheet that was posted in the dining hall each night. Jobs were alternated on the kibbutz, and Ben-Gurion had to laugh when he saw his first job—carrying manure! When the manager asked what name he wanted to be called, Ben-Gurion answered, "Call me David."

David worked diligently at whatever duties he was assigned, constantly struggling not to show his fatigue. He

Upon retirement from public life in 1953, Ben-Gurion moved to a kibbutz at Sdeh Boker in the desert. He worked at farm tasks, including tending the sheep, his favorite job.

never complained, even when he hurt his back tending sheep or when the temperature went above one hundred degrees. Within a short time, David's enthusiasm and co-operation put the kibbutzniks at ease. Paula bustled about the communal kitchen, giving the kibbutzniks cooking hints and health tips. Her warmth further endeared the Ben-Gurions to the kibbutzniks. They started thinking of him more as a friend than as the prime minister of Israel.

At Sdeh Boker, Ben-Gurion grew more relaxed than he had been in years, even allowing his sense of humor to emerge. He talked to the kibbutz teenagers, asking their opinions and listening to their answers. He started writing his memoirs, as well as a book about Israel's history, so that young generations of Jews could learn about their Jewish heritage.

David's favorite job on the kibbutz was tending sheep. He fed and cleaned them, tied their legs together to weigh them, and, when necessary, bottle-fed the baby sheep. He grew so attached to the lambs that whenever one of his cabinet members visited him he would show them off as if they were his children. Ben-Gurion felt as if he were in another world at Sdeh Boker. In the spring of 1954, the kibbutzniks saw the first results of their labors. Tomatoes, corn, sunflowers, and watermelons grew out of the desert soil. David felt he could stay at Sdeh Boker forever. Unfortunately, fate had other plans for David Ben-Gurion.

TEN

★

The Prophet Returns

Ben-Gurion had enjoyed half of his leave of absence when two crises called him back to Jerusalem. First, Nasser demanded that Great Britain vacate its military base in the Suez Canal Zone, and the British had agreed. Nasser planned to take over Great Britain's vacated military installations and make an all-out attack against Israel. In the meantime, he refused to let Israeli goods pass through the Suez Canal, and blockaded Israel's southern sea outlet through the Gulf of Aqaba and the Tiran Straits, which was a violation of international law. In addition, the Arab League blacklisted any ship or company doing business with Israel.

The second crisis, called the "Lavon Affair," was related to the first, as it involved an Israeli spy plot to keep the British in the Canal Zone. The "Lavon Affair" would become the biggest scandal in Israel's history.

Without consulting his superiors, Benjamin Gibli, Israel's chief of intelligence, ordered the leader of an Israeli spy ring to bomb Arab and American property in Egypt.

Gibli reasoned that Nasser would think an Arab extremist group was responsible and order Egyptian troops to attack them. The extremist group would then retaliate against Nasser's soldiers, and Great Britain would stay in the Canal Zone, not about to leave while a civil war raged in Egypt.

On Gibli's orders, the Israeli spy leader checked into a hotel room in Cairo in late June 1954. He turned on the "Voice of Israel" radio station, and when he heard the announcer give a recipe for English tea cake, he knew the signal to start the bombings had been given. On July 2, two Jews bombed a post office in Alexandria. On July 14 and 22, Israeli spies went into movie theaters in Cairo and Alexandria, ripped open the seats, and left eyeglass cases containing bombs inside the torn seats. One spy's case exploded in his pocket on his way into the theater. Egyptian police arrested him. Shortly afterward the police arrested other members of the Israeli spy ring, and the story made the newspapers.

Gibli had previously told Israeli chief of staff, Moshe Dayan, and Pinhas Lavon, acting defense minister, about his plan. Dayan had rejected it, and there is no evidence that Lavon, a man disliked by the Knesset for his insults and snubs of fellow members, agreed to the plan. When Lavon asked Gibli about the Israeli arrests, Gibli said there had been an Egyptian crackdown on Jews, but said nothing about the spy plot.

On July 12, ten days after the first explosion, Moshe Dayan left to go on a tour of the United States, supposedly sponsored by the Pentagon. Yet on July 19, Gibli wrote Dayan a letter telling him about the explosions. People wondered why Gibli would write Dayan about explosions that occurred while he was still in Israel. In August 1954, Dayan went to Sdeh Boker and told Ben-Gurion that Pinhas Lavon gave the go-ahead signal for the bombings. Ben-Gurion chose to believe Dayan, since an inquiry might reveal that Dayan or another member of the army gave the signal, which would damage the army's good name.

Next Dayan told Gibli to say that Lavon gave the order, or Gibli would be blamed. Gibli agreed, and he, Dyan, and Gibli's secretary doctored all records concerning the case. In Gibli's letter to Dayan, the secretary added the phrase "as Lavon has instructed" to the sentence telling Dayan the bombings had begun. All mention of the first two bombings were erased from the records. On November 1, Gibli charged Lavon with giving the go-ahead signal. Lavon was outraged and asked for a Knesset investigation. At the same time, he demanded that he be allowed to reorganize the Defense Ministry and fire his enemies. Moshe Sharett, acting prime minister, refused, and Lavon resigned. The Lavon Affair was closed—or so it seemed.

On February 21, 1955, Ben-Gurion returned to his seat in the Knesset, and in July he was reelected prime minister. Ben-Gurion sincerely wanted to make peace with the Arabs. "Nasser can have peace in five minutes," he said. "All he has to do is telephone, and I will see him anywhere, any time."[1] Nasser did not phone.

Late that year, the Soviet bloc countries made an arms pact with Egypt and Syria. For the rest of the year, Arabs and Jews fought an undeclared war of nightly skirmishes. Then in July 1956, Nasser nationalized the Suez Canal, announcing that the canal belonged to Egypt and that its international operators must leave.

In the middle of the Arab-Israeli conflict, the world's attention was drawn from Middle East tension to Russian aggression, as the Soviet Union crushed the Hungarian rebellion and occupied Hungary. Ben-Gurion decided now was his chance to act. He made an agreement with Great Britain and France to help Israel fight the Arabs. On October 29, in a surprise attack, an Israeli paratroop battalion dropped within striking distance of the Suez Canal, and defeated Egyptian forces there. The United Nations Security Council called for a cease-fire.

As Ben-Gurion had hoped, Nasser refused. Then, according to the Israeli agreement with Great Britain and

France, their air forces bombed the Egyptian airfields. Moshe Dayan led a battalion to join the paratroopers, and in five days, the two forces cleared out all fedayeen commando bases. The Israelis now occupied the Gaza Strip, the city of Sharm El Sheikh, and most of the Sinai Peninsula. Thus the Straits of Tiran were reopened to Israeli shipping.

During the fighting, the Soviet Union threatened to aid Egypt with missiles if Israel and her allies did not stop attacks against the Arabs. The United States promised to retaliate against the Soviets if they bombed Britain or France, but in its desire not to antagonize Arab oil suppliers, made no similar offer to Israel. Yet in spite of the United States offer of support, Great Britain and France gave in to the Russian threat.

Ben-Gurion refused to be threatened by the Soviets. He announced that the Sinai War was ". . . the greatest and most glorious military operation in the annals of our people. . . ."[2] The United Nations General Assembly, however, felt otherwise. Its members passed a resolution ordering Israeli forces out of the Sinai. Ben-Gurion refused, unless the United Nations guaranteed both an end to Arab raids across the Gaza Strip, and Israeli ships' rights to use the Straits of Tiran. The Security Council agreed, and posted United Nations Emergency Forces (UNEF) to patrol the area.

Israel's military victory gave hope to other small nations that they, too, could win wars against enemies twice their

The growing crisis with Egypt forced Ben-Gurion out of retirement in 1955 when he resumed his duties as Prime Minister. Here he is shown conferring with Major General Moshe Dayan following the successful military campaign in the Sinai peninsula in November, 1956.

size. Citizens from small nations such as Ghana, Nigeria, and Cambodia traveled to Israel for training in Israeli military tactics. In addition, these people studied Israeli methods of farming, education, and building industries.

Ben-Gurion rejoiced that his goal for Israel to become an inspiration to the world, a "light unto the nations," was finally bearing its first fruit. After the Sinai War, as the conflict was called, Jews hailed Ben-Gurion as a hero and pushed him even higher atop his pedestal. Unfortunately, David Ben-Gurion did not realize that heroes who live on pedestals often fall off.

In 1956, while Egypt joined Syria, Lebanon, and Iraq to form the United Arab Republic, in the Knesset the different political parties still refused to unite. Ben-Gurion grew even more annoyed by the parties' disunity, which was blocking his efforts to pass measures that he felt were vital for Israel's growth as a nation. He decided the only solution was to get more young leaders, like Abba Eban, Moshe Dayan, and Shimon Peres, to join Mapai. He believed the younger generation would agree with his progressive measures and outvote the smaller political parties.

When he announced his views at a party conference, many Mapai veterans were hurt that Ben-Gurion seemed to think they were too old to perform their duties. In addition, the veterans feared this "new blood" would take over their positions in Mapai. At the same time, the younger leaders had their own complaints against Ben-Gurion. Moshe Dayan had retired as chief of staff, hoping that Ben-Gurion would nominate him for a cabinet post. But Ben-Gurion, angry with Dayan for opposing the Sinai peace treaty, told him he was not yet ready for the job. In response, Moshe Dayan opened a Pandora's box that Ben-Gurion thought had been closed years before.

By 1959, Pinhas Lavon was secretary-general of the Histadrut general federation of labor. At a Mapai convention, he demanded to be allowed to reorganize the Histadrut to give him equal power with state economic leaders. Moshe

Dayan objected to Lavon's request by yelling at him. The meeting turned into chaos as the two men shouted insults at each other. The Mapai party became infused with suspicion and hatred. Much of the scorn was directed at Ben-Gurion, who adamantly supported Moshe Dayan.

Golda Myerson, who had changed her last name to Meir in 1956 at Ben-Gurion's insistence that all his ministers choose Hebrew surnames, had her own complaints about Ben-Gurion. He had named her foreign minister, yet he always asked Moshe Dayan and Shimon Peres to handle all major foreign negotiations. When Golda complained, Ben-Gurion would promise to let her handle all future foreign negotiations, then never keep his promise. As a result, Golda, who had idolized Ben-Gurion since she was a teenager, became Ben-Gurion's major opposition in his "new blood" plan.

In the 1959 national elections, however, Ben-Gurion managed to capture enough votes for Mapai that his party won its largest majority since 1948. Moshe Dayan became minister of agriculture, and Abba Eben minister of education. Ben-Gurion was at the peak of his power, but someone was waiting in the wings to usurp his power, and remove him from his lofty position on his pedestal.

Ben-Gurion's fall from power began one afternoon in February 1960, when a military intelligence officer paid a visit to Pinhas Lavon. The officer told Lavon that he felt guilty for obeying his superior's orders to keep silent during the 1954 Israeli spy plot, and he now wanted to tell Lavon the truth. Afterward, Lavon angrily confronted Ben-Gurion, who agreed to form a two-man investigative committee. But the committee would determine only whether former Chief of Intelligence Gibli was guilty of forgery, not whether Lavon gave the go-ahead signal for the bombings.

On another afternoon a short time later, while the committee investigated the Lavon Affair, Ben-Gurion was listening to the radio when a special news report interrupted his program. Adolf Eichmann, who had played a leading role in Hitler's execution of Jews, had been spotted in Buenos Aires, Argentina. Eichmann, like many other Nazis, had presumably fled to South America when the Allies invaded Berlin. On May 13, acting on Ben-Gurion's orders, Israeli agents kidnapped Eichmann in Buenos Aires and smuggled him into Israel. Eichmann was tried for committing "war crimes" (murdering Jews or other minorities during the Holocaust), found guilty, and hanged. Many people criticized Ben-Gurion for the kidnapping, and in Argentina violent acts of anti-Semitism erupted.

In October, the two-man committee still had not reached a decision concerning the Lavon Affair, and Pinhas Lavon demanded that Ben-Gurion clear him immediately. When Ben-Gurion refused, Lavon informed the Foreign Affairs and Security Committee, and someone leaked the story to the press. Moshe Sharett, angry at Ben-Gurion for forcing his resignation as prime minister after Ben-Gurion returned from Sdeh Boker, announced he would defend Lavon. With Sharett's support, Lavon considered his name cleared and agreed to drop the case.

Ben-Gurion, however, demanded that a judicial committee try the case so the army's reputation would be cleared from involvement with the 1954 Israeli spy plot. His advisers warned him that a public trial would cause a national crisis. A compromise was reached in which a seven-man committee would review the evidence and make a recommendation only, not a judgment of Lavon's guilt or innocence.

Yet in December, the committee judged Lavon innocent, based upon a confession by Gibli's secretary that she had forged the reports. Ben-Gurion raged that the committee was not authorized to make a judgment. In February 1961, he threatened to resign if the Knesset did not fire Lavon from the Histadrut. Ben-Gurion's colleagues, still believing that Israel could not survive without him, voted to oust Lavon. Non-Mapai members of the Knesset resigned in protest, and many Israelis grew disillusioned with Ben-

Gurion for causing Lavon's resignation without first proving him guilty. The new elections reflected their feelings, and Mapai lost five seats in the Knesset.

The Lavon Affair grew into a cancerous tumor of rage inside Ben-Gurion. His mind began to weaken, and he started acting as old as his chronological years—seventy-four. He lost track of his thoughts in the middle of sentences, he repeated himself, and often could not remember who held what positions in the cabinet.

When Yitzhak Ben-Zvi died in April 1963, Ben-Gurion fell into deep despair. Two months later, he again stunned Israel by retiring as prime minister and defense minister, although he kept his seat in the Knesset. He chose Levi Eshkol, former economics adviser, as his successor. For the first time, members of the Knesset did not beg Ben-Gurion to stay. He spent the next year at Sdeh Boker rereading the Lavon Affair reports. In October 1964, he again demanded that a judicial committee try the case. Levi Eshkol refused. In addition, Eshkol reinstated Lavon into Mapai. Then, two cabinet members who had been studying the Lavon Affair agreed with Ben-Gurion's request. Eshkol threatened to resign if Mapai held a judicial inquiry, and the party backed him. An outraged Ben-Gurion resigned from Mapai.

At Sdeh Boker, Paula threw away Ben-Gurion's hate mail, kept reporters at bay, and begged his few remaining friends to convince him to make up with Eshkol. At a Mapai convention in 1965, all the members criticized Ben-Gurion ruthlessly. Moshe Sharett declared, "We must ask Ben-Gurion either to forsake the issue and join the mainstream of our life or to relinquish the crown of leadership."[3]

In June, Ben-Gurion announced he intended to run a new slate of candidates from members within Mapai. The party, tired of Ben-Gurion's temper tantrums, expelled him. In retaliation, he formed a new party from his few remaining supporters, called "Rafi," or the "Israeli Workers' List." Then Ben-Gurion announced he was available to be elected prime minister. Mapai countered by expelling all members supporting Rafi, and in November, Rafi won only ten seats in the Knesset. In 1966, when the new Knesset building opened in Jerusalem, Ben-Gurion was not asked to speak at the opening day ceremonies. He was deeply hurt and refused to attend.

In October, the Jewish nation celebrated Ben-Gurion's eightieth birthday by having a month-long series of pageants in his honor. In mid-October, ten thousand Israelis traveled to Sdeh Boker for a special celebration. Israeli flags stood along the paths to the kibbutz, and kleig lights swept their giant beams over the gathering. Ten thousand voices sang, "Happy Birthday, Ben-Gurion!" While he appreciated the tribute, Ben-Gurion felt alone in the huge crowd. Not one of his old friends had come.

ELEVEN

✦

The End of the Giant Killer

In May 1967, Nasser forced the United Nations Emergency Forces to withdraw from the armistice lines established after the Sinai War, and Egyptian troops blockaded the Straits of Tiran. Then Syria stationed troops along Israel's borders. In response, Prime Minister Eshkol mobilized a unit of the Israeli Defense Forces. Army Chief of Staff Yitzhak Rabin went to Sdeh Boker to ask Ben-Gurion's advice. Ben-Gurion said that Nasser's actions were not cause enough to wage another war. Rabin left feeling deeply saddened that Ben-Gurion seemed to have lost his fighting spirit.

While the Israelis' image of Ben-Gurion as a giant-killer grew dimmer, their perception of Moshe Dayan as a strong leader grew larger. When Mapai leaders urged Dayan to take over as defense minister, Ben-Gurion suggested that Dayan become prime minister as well. Dayan agreed, but only if Ben-Gurion would come to Tel Aviv and advise him on military strategy. Ben-Gurion, happy that his protégé wanted his advice, consented, and he and Paula moved into his old apartment in Tel Aviv.

On May 26, Nasser held a press conference and declared that Egypt wanted to fight Israel, but he was waiting for the right day when the Egyptian army would be fully prepared. Moshe Dayan, in his new position as defense minister, did not want to wait for Nasser to make up his mind when was the right day for the Arabs to destroy Israel. On June 5, Dayan ordered the Israeli Defense Forces to attack Egypt. In three hours, the Israelis all but destroyed Egypt's aircraft, which was parked on their airfields waiting for Nasser to give the order to attack.

By June 10, six days later, Israel occupied huge portions of Arab territory, and the "Six-Day War" was virtually over. The Jews' most cherished conquest during the war was the Old City of Jerusalem, which the Arabs had occupied since 1948. Now the Jews could once again pray at the Western Wall and live in the city that most represented their history.

Israel's victory seemed to light a fire within Ben-Gurion, and he regained some of his old fighting spirit. At eighty-one years old, he flew to every front to visit "his troops." On the other hand, during the war Ben-Gurion had waited for Moshe Dayan to ask his advice, but Dayan never once called on him. It has been suggested that Dayan never intended to ask Ben-Gurion's advice, but made the request merely to coax Ben-Gurion into suggesting that Dayan become prime minister.

After the war, the UN Security Council proposed a peace settlement in which Israel would give up all Arab territory captured during the war. Moshe Dayan insisted upon direct negotiations with the Arabs. They refused, and no peace treaty was signed.

In December 1967, when Ben-Gurion's former Rafi party joined with Mapai and the Ahdut HaAvodah labor union party to form a single "Labor Alignment party," Ben-Gurion felt even more cast out by his colleagues. He had fought for labor unity all his life. And now, when his efforts had finally paid off, he was excluded from participating in the achievement. He made one last attempt to regain his power by forming another political party, called the "State List." His attempt failed, however, as the State List soon merged with the Labor Alignment party.

David Ben-Gurion had finally fallen off his pedestal. Jews were sad, but no longer terrified, to lose their giant killer. Israel had matured in the past twenty years, and Jews no longer believed they needed Ben-Gurion to protect them from their enemies. The age of Messiahs had passed.

In January 1968, Ben-Gurion's personal life fell apart as well. Paula, at the age of seventy-six, suffered a brain hemorrhage and died. Ben-Gurion was overcome by grief and guilt for neglecting her so much during their marriage. He had even, at the doctor's insistence, left Paula in her last hours of life. Had she asked for him? He squeezed her lifeless hands and, for one of the few times since his mother died, David Ben-Gurion cried out loud.

Paula was buried on a hilltop overlooking Sdeh Boker. But it took Ben-Gurion a long time to believe that she had actually died. Often he would say, "Excuse me," when getting up from the dinner table, only to remember suddenly that Paula was not sitting across from him anymore.

Ben-Gurion missed Paula's shrill voice ordering him to "Take a sweater. You'll catch cold." Or shouting at visitors to "Go away! Ben-Gurion needs his rest." He wished he had been a more loving husband, but it was too late now. Paula's death made him realize it was also too late to change his life's course from a sole commitment to Zionism into a life including commitment to his family and colleagues as well.

Yet strangely, just as Ben-Gurion's mother's death caused him to build a shield around his emotions, Paula's death seemed to destroy that shield. A friend of Paula's said, "Ben-Gurion became more sentimental and human. No one believed he would grieve so much. No one thought he was capable of it."[1]

He even started spending more time with his children, and developed a deep love for his grandchildren and two great-grandchildren. He was suddenly filled with an overwhelming desire to participate in their young lives. Ben-Gurion read to them, played games with them, and told them stories about the rebuilding of Israel. One night, his grandson Yariv was astonished when he came home to find a beaming Ben-Gurion, who had been baby-sitting, on the floor giggling and rolling around with Yariv's son.

In his eighties, Ben-Gurion was also able to spend more time with Rachel, whose husband had died several years earlier. Rachel, at age seventy-eight, had grown old. She was terribly thin, and her face had become pale and wrinkled. The two would meet at Ben-Gurion's home, where they would sit in his living room and talk, mostly about the past.

From Sdeh Boker, Ben-Gurion kept up with the many changes occurring in the Middle East. In February 1969, Prime Minister Levi Eshkol died, and Golda Meir became prime minister. In Egypt, Gamal Abdel Nasser died and was succeeded by Anwar el-Sadat, the speaker and vice president of the United Arab Republic National Assembly. Sadat pledged to continue Nasser's anti-Jewish policies by denying recognition of Israel, and by refusing to negotiate a peace treaty with the Jewish state.

In October, Ben-Gurion celebrated his eighty-third birthday. His memory lapses had grown worse, and he was unaware that he repeated himself. In 1970, Ben-Gurion gave up his seat in the Knesset for good and retired to Sdeh Boker, saying he wanted to be a private citizen. As Israel welcomed her three millionth immigrant, David Ben-Gurion ended his political career of more than sixty years of service to Israel.

At Sdeh Boker, even though Ben-Gurion was seeing Rachel in person, he started writing her letters. In one, he said, "I presume that you know well how precious you have been to me since our youth."[2] In another, he spoke of his dream, saying, "There is hope, dear Rachel, that peace is

David Ben-Gurion retired once more to Sdeh Boker
in the 1960s. He spent most of his last years in
his library working on his memoirs or sharing his
thoughts about world affairs with visiting journalists,
students, and dignitaries.

approaching, not quickly, but slowly, slowly, and . . . it appears to me that by the end of this century the prophecy of Isaiah will be fulfilled."[3]

When he was not spending time with Rachel, Ben-Gurion worked on finishing his book, *Israel, A Personal History*. In the book, Ben-Gurion said: "For our security, survival, and status in the world . . . Israel must strive incessantly for moral, cultural, technological, and social improvement and to be a unique people."[4]

Before she died, Paula had urged Ben-Gurion to make up with his colleagues in the Knesset. For the second time in three years, however, death made it impossible for Ben-Gurion to make amends for his neglectful, often rude, behavior toward someone else. Levi Eshkol and Moshe Sharett had died, and Ben-Gurion could not honor Paula's last wishes. He decided to write letters of apology to the rest of his former colleagues and ask for their friendship. He even wrote to Pinhas Lavon.

Ben-Gurion's political enemies accepted his apologies, and in return gave him a special luncheon honoring his eighty-fifth birthday. Yet afterward, they again forgot he existed and focused their attention on the Arabs, who were expanding their attacks to include Jews living outside Israel.

On May 30, 1972, Lebanese-trained, Japanese terrorists stormed the Lydda Airport and shot twenty-seven people, most of them Puerto Rican pilgrims. At the Olympic Games, held in Munich that year, Arab guerrillas raided the Israeli athletes' dormitory. By means of satellite television, the world watched in horror as the guerrillas killed eleven Israeli athletes.

At Sdeh Boker, Ben-Gurion was thinking that Knesset members had hit him with all the painful ammunition in their stores, when the following year they shot him down again. In May 1973, at the celebration of Israel's twenty-fifth anniversary as a state, Prime Minister Golda Meir did not ask Ben-Gurion to give a speech or even to sit on the speakers' platform. Instead he was assigned a seat in the audience.

On October 6, 1973, most of the world's Jews were in synagogues participating in their most holy day of the year, *Yom Kippur*, the "Day of Atonement," when Jews ask God's pardon for sins committed during the past year. While Jews in Israel attended religious services, occasional explosions shook the synagogues, drowning out the cantors' chants, as the Egyptians and the Syrians launched a joint surprise attack on Israel. In the first hours of the attack, later named "The Yom Kippur War," Egyptian planes bombed the Suez Canal and the Syrians pushed the Israelis out of the Golan Heights.

After three days of Arab victories, the Israeli Defense Forces finally came out of shock. Within two weeks, the Israelis recaptured every Israeli settlement taken by the Arabs. Israel thus won its fourth war against the Arabs since 1948. The United Nations drew up a cease-fire agreement. Nevertheless, the fighting continued for two more days, during which time the Israelis captured the Suez Canal Zone and cut off the Egyptian army from Cairo.

American President Richard Nixon sent Secretary of State Henry Kissinger to help the two nations negotiate a peace settlement. He proposed that Israel withdraw its troops from Egypt, but assume defensive positions in the Sinai away from the Suez Canal. The canal would be re-opened to Israeli shipping, and the United Nations Emergency Forces would patrol Arab and Israeli borders.

A meeting was held in Geneva, Switzerland, to write the formal peace treaty. While Defense Minister Moshe Dayan insisted upon a phased-out withdrawal of Israeli troops from Arab territory, President Sadat insisted that the Israelis withdraw at once to Israel's pre-1967 borders. To get Western governments to side with the Arabs, King Faisal of Saudi Arabia called for an oil embargo against Western powers. In the United States, the results of the Arab embargo could be seen daily in the gasoline lines which formed at service stations while Americans waited to "fill up" before the pumps went dry.

In Sdeh Boker, Ben-Gurion could not muster up enough

energy to get more than a little annoyed at the embargo. His strength was failing fast, and he wanted to use his remaining energy to finish writing his memoirs. During these days, his friends would find him talking to himself, mostly about a beautiful girl from Plonsk whom he had loved when he was young. Ben-Gurion never uttered her name.

On November 18, 1973, while spending some time in his Tel Aviv apartment, Ben-Gurion suffered a stroke. He was rushed to the hospital. Rachel came to be with him, and for a few days Ben-Gurion rallied. Then his condition grew worse, and his doctors asked his children to come to the hospital. Rachel, tears streaming down her cheeks, held Ben-Gurion's hand that Saturday morning, December 1, as, at 11:06 A.M. Israeli time, and 4:06 P.M. New York time, David Ben-Gurion, killer of giants, passed away.

Ben-Gurion was buried beside Paula at Sdeh Boker. Jews and non-Jews alike experienced a deep feeling of loss, and the whole world paid tribute to the man from Plonsk— farmer, statesman, soldier, hero, prophet, and creator of the Jewish state.

Before Ben-Gurion died, he completed his memoirs. He included his thoughts about what Israel means to Jews: "It is two things. An ark and a Covenant. . . . There are some who see Israel's importance primarily as an Ark, a place where the persecuted can go. . . . I think the covenant takes precedence over the concept of refuge. . . . Israel cannot just be a refuge. If it is to survive as a valid nation it has to be much, much more. . . ."[5]

According to Ben-Gurion, when God sent Moses to deliver the Ten Commandments to the Jews, He added an extra commandment, that the Jews should be *Amsagolah*. Ben-Gurion explained this Hebrew term as meaning that when God said the Jews were "chosen," He did not mean He had singled them out as special. Rather, God chose the Jews to bear an extra responsibility—that of showing the world human kindness, morality, and justice by their own actions.

For David Ben-Gurion, time ran out before he saw Israel set this example of humanity to the world. He left the fulfillment of that dream as a legacy to the Jews who remained behind, hoping that one day each one of them would become truly *Amsagolah*. Then Israel would burst into the flame that David Ben-Gurion believed God intended when he declared to the Jews:

I have called thee in righteousness . . .
and set thee for a Covenant of the people,
for a light unto the nations.

Isaiah: 42:6

Notes

CHAPTER ONE

1. Gertrude Samuels, *Ben-Gurion: Fighter of Goliaths* (New York: Crowell, 1974), p. 25.
2. Ibid., p. 37.
3. Maurice Edelman, *The Story of David Ben-Gurion* (New York: G. P. Putnam's Sons, 1964), p. 25.
4. Daniel Kurzman, *Ben-Gurion: Prophet of Fire* (New York: Simon & Schuster, 1983), p. 53.
5. Ibid., p. 71.
6. Samuels, *Ben-Gurion: Fighter of Goliaths*, p. 38.
7. David Ben-Gurion, *Memoirs*; comp. Thomas R. Bransten (New York: World Publishing, 1970), p. 1 of Preface.
8. Ibid., p. 180.
9. Mollie Keller, *Golda Meir* (New York: Franklin Watts, 1983), p. 23.
10. Kurzman, *Ben-Gurion: Prophet of Fire*, p. 57.
11. Ibid., p. 63.

CHAPTER TWO

1. David Ben-Gurion, *Memoirs*, comp. Thomas R. Bransten, p. 41.
2. Michael Bar-Zohar, *Ben-Gurion* (New York: Adama Books, 1977), p. 12.
3. Kurzman, *Ben-Gurion: Prophet of Fire*, p. 84.
4. Ben-Gurion, *Memoirs*, comp. Thomas R. Bransten, p. 58.

5. Samuels, *Ben-Gurion: Fighter of Goliaths*, p. 52.
6. Ben-Gurion, *Memoirs*, comp. Thomas R. Bransten, p. 58.
7. Ibid., p. 60.
8. Samuels, *Ben-Gurion: Fighter of Goliaths*, p. 59.
9. Michael Bar-Zohar, *Ben-Gurion: The Armed Prophet* (Englewood Cliffs, N.J.: Prentice-Hall, 1968), p. 26.

CHAPTER THREE

1. Kurzman, *Ben-Gurion: Prophet of Fire*, p. 114.
2. Ibid., p. 117.
3. Samuels, *Ben-Gurion: Fighter of Goliaths*, p. 62.
4. Ibid., p. 71.
5. Ibid., p. 64.

CHAPTER FOUR

1. Kurzman, *Ben-Gurion: Prophet of Fire*, p. 139.
2. Ibid., p. 146.

CHAPTER FIVE

1. Samuels, *Ben-Gurion: Fighter of Goliaths*, p. 88.
2. Ibid., p. 88.
3. Kurzman, *Ben-Gurion: Prophet of Fire*, p. 164.
4. Ibid., p. 164.
5. Ibid., p. 189.

CHAPTER SIX

1. Bar-Zohar, *Ben-Gurion*, p. 87.
2. Ibid., p. 93.
3. Samuels, *Ben-Gurion: Fighter of Goliaths*, p. 97.
4. Kurzman, *Ben-Gurion: Prophet of Fire*, p. 216.
5. Ibid., p. 217.
6. Samuels, *Ben-Gurion: Fighter of Goliaths*, p. 105.
7. Ibid., p. 105.
8. Kurzman, *Ben-Gurion: Prophet of Fire*, p. 225.

CHAPTER SEVEN

1. Samuels, *Ben-Gurion: Fighter of Goliaths*, p. 107.
2. Edelman, *David, The Story of David Ben-Gurion*, p. 123.
3. Samuels, *Ben-Gurion: Fighter of Goliaths*, p. 111.
4. Ibid., p. 111.
5. Ibid., p. 113.
6. Kurzman, *Ben-Gurion: Prophet of Fire*, p. 275.

CHAPTER EIGHT

1. Samuels, *Ben-Gurion: Fighter of Goliaths*, p. 138.
2. David Ben-Gurion, *Memoirs*, comp. Thomas R. Bransten, p. 87.
3. Kurzman, *Ben-Gurion: Prophet of Fire*, p. 299.
4. Edelman, *David, The Story of David Ben-Gurion*, p. 157.
5. Samuels, *Ben-Gurion: Fighter of Goliaths*, p. 165.

CHAPTER NINE

1. Kurzman, *Ben-Gurion: Prophet of Fire*, p. 402.
2. David Ben-Gurion, *Memoirs*, comp. Thomas R. Bransten, p. 256.
3. Kurzman, *Ben-Gurion: Prophet of Fire*, p. 337.
4. Samuels, *Ben-Gurion: Fighter of Goliaths*, p. 8.
5. Ibid., p. 10.

CHAPTER TEN

1. Samuels, *Ben-Gurion: Fighter of Goliaths*, p. 208.
2. Kurzman, *Ben-Gurion: Prophet of Fire*, p. 394.
3. Ibid., p. 447.

CHAPTER ELEVEN

1. Kurzman, *Ben-Gurion: Prophet of Fire*, p. 394.
2. Ibid., p. 456.
3. Ibid., p. 458.
4. Ibid., p. 459.
5. David Ben-Gurion, *Memoirs*, comp. Thomas R. Bransten, p. 175–76.

✡ For Further Reading

Ben-Gurion, David. *Israel: Years of Challenge*. New York: Holt, Rinehart, and Winston, 1963.

Cameron, James. *The Making of Israel*. New York: Taplinger Publishing Co., 1977.

Ellis, Harry B. *Israel: One Land, Two Peoples*. New York: Crowell, 1972.

Goldstone, Robert. *Next Year in Jerusalem*. Boston: Atlantic Monthly Press, 1978.

Gordon, Thomas. *Voyage of the Damned*. New York: Stein & Day, 1974.

Porter, Katherine Anne. *Ship of Fools*. Boston: Little, Brown, 1962.

Uris, Leon. *Exodus*. New York: Doubleday, 1958.

Uris, Leon. *Mila 18*. New York: Doubleday, 1961.

Uris, Leon. *Q.B. VII*. New York: Doubleday, 1970.

Index

Abdullah, King, 81, 87
Adenauer, Konrad, 98
Afrika Korps, 73–74
Ahdut (journal), 30–31, 33
Ahdut HaAvodah, 43–44, 47–48,
    56, 58, 114
American Jews, 35–40, 75–77, 81,
    95
Anti-Semitism, 18, 21, 60–61, 63
Anti-Zionists, 38–39
Arab-Israeli conflict, 84–91
Arabs, 30, 65
    and control of Palestine, 44,
        70–71
    invasion of Israel by, 86–87
    oil interests of, 57
    and Jerusalem, 46–47
    See also Jewish-Arab relations
Arlosoff, Chaim, 60

Balfour Declaration, 40, 44, 46–49,
    70–71
Battle of Jerusalem, 87–88
Begin, Menachem, 74, 77, 79,
    88–89, 95, 98

Ben-Gurion, David, 12–17
    in America, 36–45
    arrest of, 35
    children of, 41, 44, 49, 54–56,
        72, 83
    death of, 119–121
    education of, 15–16
    ejection from Palestine, 35
    emigration to Palestine, 22
    Eretz Israel by, 40
    family of, 13, 15–17, 22, 43,
        56, 75
    and Histadrut, 49, 51, 56–57
    and the Holocaust, 64–71
    Israel, A Personal History by,
        118
    and Jewish Agency, 61
    and Jewish Legion, 41
    and Jewish State of Israel, 19,
        72–84, 86
    and kibbutz life, 99–100, 102
    and Lavon Affair, 111
    and Mapai, 58–62
    as military strategist, 76
    in Moscow, 53

3903

Y.A
B
B-GUR
C.3

DATE DUE

1/7/04			

HIGHSMITH 45-220